THE POTTER'S WORKBOOK

THE POTTER'S WORKBOOK

Christine Rowe

B. T. Batsford Ltd · London

© Christine Rowe 1992
First published 1992

Typeset by Deltatype Ltd, Ellesmere Port, Cheshire
and printed in Hong Kong

Published by B. T. Batsford Ltd
4 Fitzhardinge Street, London W1H 0AH

A catalogue record for this book is
available from the British Library

ISBN 0 7134 6619 7

Front cover photography: Stephen Brayne

Back cover
Thrown porcelain pot with crackled glaze
by Christine-Ann Richards

Contents

Acknowledgements

I am grateful to the following for permission to use illustrations of their work: Gilles Le Corre, Glen Etienne, Ewen Henderson, Mary Lambert, Suzanne Lang, Christine Ann Richards, Lucie Rie, Jacob Sutton and David Whiting on behalf of Geoffrey Whiting; and to the Ashmolean and Pitt Rivers Museums in Oxford.

The drawings and photographs are my own unless otherwise acknowledged, but special thanks are due to my students who allowed me to show their work and who are named throughout the text; to Norman Unger, my photographic adviser; and to the encouragement of my friends, family and colleagues.

Christine Rowe

Noble and original craft
Above the first,
For in the industry of clay,
God was the first potter
and man the first pot.

Anon

Introduction

If you want to know more about pottery – how to do it better, how to go about it in a more confident or systematic way, and what its parameters are – then this book is written for you.

You may already have made a start. You probably played with clay as a child, or did some pottery classes at school, and maybe you are now discovering a new method of expressing yourself in your later years.

If you have joined an adult evening class, you may want to try your hand at making pots in a more creative way or for a more formal reason. Perhaps you want to work towards an exhibition or to make a collection of pots for a college entrance portfolio. You may simply be looking for stimulation and encouragement to help you make more exciting pots which are challenging on a personal level. This workbook sets out to provide just that – to give you the confidence to make your own statements.

Examples of projects are laid out to show how ideas have come about and how they progress from start to finish through a series of design processes. These examples have been chosen to illustrate the breadth of possibilities for designing pottery, from landscapes and natural forms through to teapots. If you adopt the suggested ways of working out your designs, you will begin to see and interpret your surroundings and own unique experiences in a different, more creative and thoughtful way.

You could discover your personal sources of design by looking at collections of pots and examples of other potters' work. Or you could experiment yourself with materials tests, re-interpreting visual materials collected while travelling. Using the given examples as a model, you can apply the same methodology to design projects of your own choosing and style. Further suggestions are made and ideas for different projects, other than those illustrated, are given throughout the book, but as guidelines not hard rules. Use these to stimulate your own original contributions to the fascinating study of the ancient medium of clay colours and glazes.

Above all, don't worry if everything does not seem to be going according to plan. You may need another person to act the role of mentor, not necessarily to tell you what to do but to discuss with you how you would like to see your work developing. This person might be a friend or partner, a teacher or another potter who can encourage, question and review your creative development.

1
Design materials
and processes

It can be useful to think about design as a series of processes from which your practical work will emerge. Each process has a system, a vocabulary and a value of its own to explore. In developing your work, the processes of **drawing**, **research** and directly **experimenting** with the clay materials are worth looking at in more detail.

3 The design table, with drawing equipment

4 Ceramics sketchbooks by Eiman Hamed, Hugh Overton and Hon Pong Lee

Drawing

To design and develop your work, you will need to explore as wide a variety of drawing media as you can collect for yourself. There are many more drawing materials available to you than the ubiquitous pencil.

Materials and tools

Any material that makes or leaves a mark can be used to design – from pastels to home-made charcoal pieces from a bonfire, from conté crayons to ink, pen and brush wash. Try to use as many different materials as you can lay your hands on and notice how each one affects your designs differently. A set of fibre tip pens and watercolours are probably the basic minimum; both are portable and also versatile.

As well as the drawing media, collect together such drawing tools as rubbers, rulers, sketchbooks of various sizes, paper of various colours and qualities, an assortment of pens and sable brushes, a camera with long and close-up lenses, display books with plastic sheets, books for cuttings, and craft knives for cutting and shaping crayons.

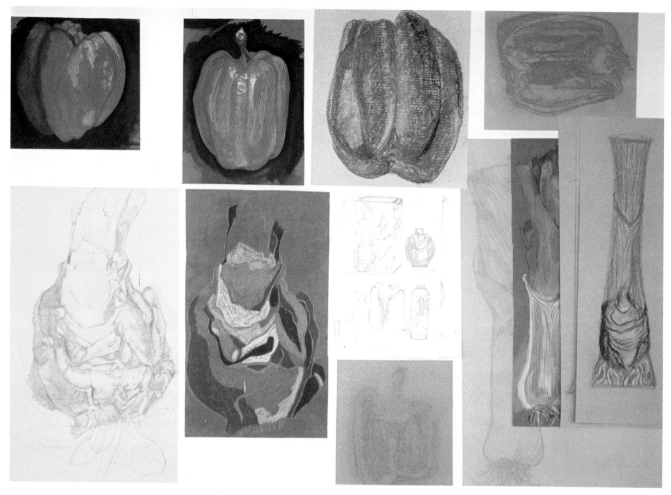

Linear drawings

Paul Klee is credited with saying that 'A line is the shortest distance between two points.' Linear drawings are made from all manner of lines and from all manner of media. Suggestions are given in each chapter.

Tonal drawings

Take some time to fully explore your drawing media to make marks other than lines, for example, dots, scribbles and washes. The way you make marks on the page helps show the texture and quality of an object. Tones can be light or dark, mottled or smooth. They are a way of expressing the form of an object and perhaps indicating how it might feel if you could pick it up.

The Italians, who contributed significantly to artistic vocabulary, gave us *chiaroscuro*, the study of light and dark – a particularly expressive way of conceiving a tonal drawing.

5 Student drawings in a variety of media, from pastels to very soft pencil

Form

Consider the difference between a circle and a ball. The former has height and width, the latter height, width and depth. How you draw this third dimension of depth indicates the solidity and weight of the object. An acceptable way to show form is by indicating shadow using *tone*. There are basically two types of shadow: *'cast' shadow*, which is thrown by the object and is often drawn underneath it to anchor it to the ground; and *'form' shadow*, which indicates the action of light upon the object and is drawn in a manner that shows surface texture.

Space

This might be defined as the areas on a drawing occupied by the composition of forms and also the spaces in

6 A collection of shells from many countries

between. 'Negative' space is a crucially important part of any drawing.

Texture

This describes the surface and also the composition of an object. How to draw it will take all your ingenuity in inventing ways to make representative marks. Collage and cut-outs could also have a role to play.

Scale and proportion

These refer to the relationship of one set of forms to another. Alteration of scale and proportion is a simple way to convert your drawings into designs. Pop art has many good examples, for example, Andy Warhol's soup cans.

References

The value of drawing is its contribution to your visual literacy, powers of observation and skill in interpreting what you see.

Notice how other designers manipulate their drawing materials to produce good drawings. Study the art of the past in your local and national galleries. Books and exhibitions give valuable opportunities to analyse how experienced artists through the ages have attempted to solve the problems of drawing, from skin texture to the movement of the wind. Look out for reproductions of the sketchbooks of Leonardo da Vinci from the sixteenth century and the sketchbooks of Picasso from the twentieth century. Visit exhibitions at your nearest art college to see what might be happening in the future.

Research

Research will help you learn about the art of the past, as well as current innovations. It will clarify your understanding of ceramics, ancient and modern. Look about you to see what is there, then pursue what interests you by fact-finding, visiting, travelling, reading, asking questions, interviewing people, etc. Follow your nose, but keep a record of what you discover.

Learn to recognize the difference between primary and secondary source materials. Primary source materials are those where you work from original sources – a plant, a figure or the view in front of you. Secondary source materials are where some of the visual decisions have already been made, for example, in a photograph of a plant, a figure or a landscape. These can be a rich source of stimulation to the creative imagination.

Primary and secondary sources both have a value, but notice how much or how little control you are able to exercise over the development of your designs because of different aspects of these sources and what has already been decided.

The length of time you spend researching a particular project could be fixed, for example, finding out how to make a teapot, or many years could be spent studying such vessels in a variety of cultures.

Where you carry out your research will depend on your personal resources of time, energy and commitment. At home you will have family, neighbours and friends, books, magazines, interior and exterior surroundings, personal collections, objects, and all the paraphernalia of daily life.

If you have access to an educational institution, there may be specialist staff and a reference library with books, magazines, slides, videos and a photocopier, plus other students for stimulus and encouragement. Your local town may have a museum with pottery and other collections, and an art gallery or exhibition space. It will certainly have streets and maybe parks – altogether a rich variety of visual experience.

Record-keeping

How you record your research deserves some thought, including what it is to be used for and future accessibility. The physical presence of your records might also encourage or discourage your creativity. Here are suggestions:

1 A sketchbook or visual diary based on a particular topic, for example, the development of landscape and natural forms.

2 A collection of photographs taken when travelling.

3 A scrapbook of cut-outs of faces and figures from magazines and newspapers. Collect pictures of young and old people, men and women, different races, active and passive compositions, etc.

4 A basket of found objects from the countryside – pebbles, rocks, dried flowers, leaves, nuts, etc.

5 Drawings made in museums of patterns from a particular culture, for example, Celtic knotwork, African batiks, Islamic calligraphy.

6 A display book with plastic sheets, containing photographs of your pots and ceramic experiments with a brief description of the clays, glazes and firings used.

7 A set of slides showing your visual stimuli, maquettes

7 *A collection of pottery tools, purchased and home-made*

and completed projects in sequence. House it in a slide carousel for easy storage and use.

8 A portfolio of mounted sketches and drawings showing a series of projects and their briefs.

9 A box of numbered but loose glaze tests, and a book with the recipes and notes for each one.

10 A box containing beachcombings and objects altered by seas and rivers.

11 A plastic sack full of interesting urban detritus – bits of motors, plastic fitments, etc.

12 Notebooks of quotations, addresses, colour recipes, ceramic vocabulary, etc.

13 A sketchbook exploring an unfamiliar medium. Show how it combines with other media.

14 A sketchbook recording your thoughts, explorations and the progress of a particular project, from start to finish.

15 A box file of catalogues, diagrams, photographs, observations and sketches of kilns of all sizes, plus fuels and countries of origin.

Experimenting with clay materials

Another important design process, as well as experimenting with drawings, is that which arises out of the clay material itself. This can come from accidental contact with clay and colours, or can be the result of hours or even years of experimentation and research. You may need no more than the clay itself, or perhaps just a recipe for it and the ingredients. You may find that your hands and the clay are enough to work with; alternatively, you may want to explore the possibilities of a whole range of equipment, or

13

just one or two specialist tools. Practical ways of directly experimenting with the clay materials are suggested in chapter 5.

The preparation for experimenting with clay often involves not only getting the materials ready, but yourself as well. Are you in the right frame of mind to explore the clay in a relaxed manner? Just as the physical activity of spiral-wedging the clay can tone up your muscles, it can act therapeutically upon your creative imagination if you allow it.

Suggested ways to start:

1 Close your eyes and explore the clay by simply squeezing it.

2 Make a hole in the middle of a ball of clay with your thumb, then pinch the wall into a small bowl.

3 Roll a ball around until you find a form that pleases you, let it dry to leather-hard, then hollow it by scooping it out from below.

4 Flatten a disc of clay against your elbow, knee or fist to make an asymmetrical bowl.

5 Press a marble-sized ball of soft clay on all the interesting textures you can find.

6 Do the same in the city, countryside or on a beach.

7 Roll out a slab of smooth clay and press objects onto it.

8 As above, then dampen the surface with a sponge and take a newsprint monoprint.

9 As **7**, but make an organized repeating pattern.

10 Roll out a slab of clay and practise slip-trailing. Cut out and keep the interesting bits.

11 Roll out a slab of clay and cut out a variety of shapes. Leave them to stiffen draped over a variety of forms and textures.

12 Roll out a slab of clay and practise angular joins, not making anything in particular to begin with but allowing the form to develop.

13 Make a pile of clay coils and arrange them in a plaster mould.

14 Roll out a smooth slab of clay and see how many different ways you can alter the surface with lines in the wet, and then the leather-hard, clay.

Maquettes

Another form of experimentation, particularly after a period of intense research, is to make maquettes or small-scale models.

A maquette is the equivalent of a sketch in relation to a painting. A sculptor might produce many maquettes before attempting a full-scale sculpture and ceramic sculptors have the same facility at their disposal. Some of the reasons for making maquettes are that they can:

- help you work out a design
- enable you to visualize a design in three-dimensional form from a two-dimensional sketch
- be used for colour testing
- be useful in testing alterations to the design
- enable further visualizations
- become a vehicle for rehearsing and refining building techniques
- provide contact with the materials and appreciation of their texture
- be useful in discovering design faults (for example, of balance) or for anticipating and correcting faults
- prevent wastage of materials if they are discovered to be inappropriate for the design
- 'stretch' time, to allow ideas to emerge and develop
- become designs in their own right (e.g. as miniatures or multiples) where repetition is the essence of an assemblage
- stimulate other work
- become a record of a larger piece of work, usefully documenting development and progression
- form a portfolio, for clients or yourself
- be easily portable when that may be important to your method of working, thinking or marketing your work
- wonderfully focus the mind from the ethereal to the practical!

8 Maquettes

Materials in the studio

In dealing with so many different activities, it is essential that you are clear what each entails so that the equipment and materials you need are to hand.

You may have no choice about where you work, but if you are organizing your studio it may be helpful to plan it like a kitchen with different workstations for each operation. Activities involving paper will need a desk, chair and good light. Does this area have to be part of the studio or would it be more practical elsewhere? Storing and weighing out dry materials will need storage bins with lids and good labels. Consult the manufacturers' recommendations about health and safety, never forgetting that *dust* is a real hazard to potters; bags of dry materials should be decanted so that a cloud of dust is not released when they are opened and closed. Accurate clear labelling is essential once you have several different bags of white powder.

Plastic clay is best stored outside in a cool place to 'weather', but smaller quantities ready for use can be kept inside in a damp condition. How will you keep your leather-hard pieces in good order? Can you make or buy a damp cupboard, or will large polythene containers with fitted lids be sufficient? How will your smaller quantities of colouring materials and oxides be stored? Check to see which are poisonous and label them accordingly. Plastic see-through containers are good. Some materials store best in a wet state; consult the manufacturers' instructions if in doubt. Glazes keep well in airtight buckets. Sieves,

glaze mops, sticks and weighing scales will all need storage with easy access.

As well as equipment, you will need shelving to hold pots which are drying, in the making, at the biscuit stage, awaiting decoration or firing, and completed for delivery or display. Can there ever be enough space or enough shelving in a pottery? Yet internationally renowned potter Lucie Rie has worked from a small basement room in west London for many years.

Site your kiln carefully for easy access, both by yourself and the service engineer. Most smaller kilns come with castors these days and are quite light and easy to manoeuvre. Kiln design changes and develops constantly so research carefully before buying a new kiln. Go to a manufacturer's demonstration day if you can, and ask other potters for their recommendations.

It is important that you wear protective clothing when you are working in the studio or you could find yourself carrying dangerous lead or silica dust around in your clothes, absorbing it through your skin or getting it into your food. Ceramic materials need to be kept carefully in order but, with sensible use, they are not harmful. Mop up spillages of glazes as soon as possible to prevent them from drying and reverting to dust.

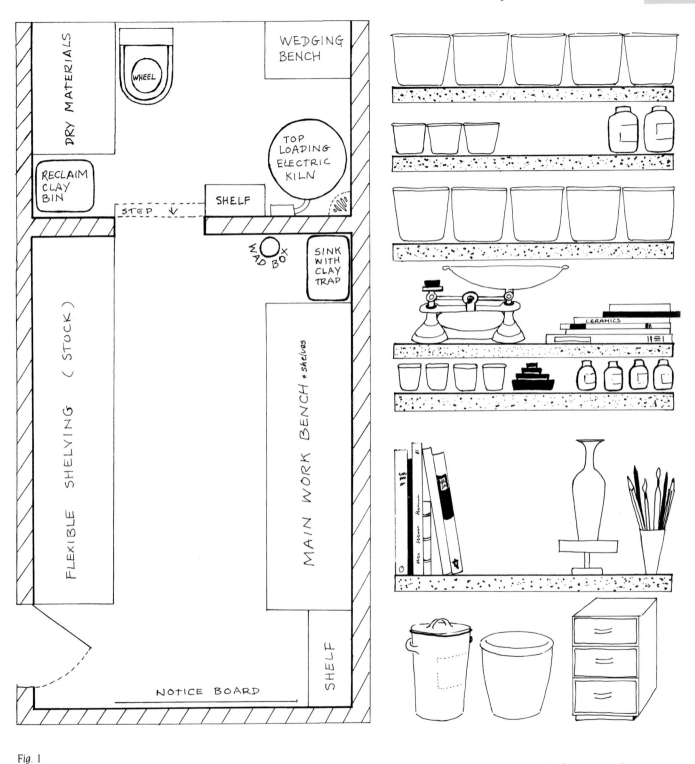

Fig. 1

-: STUDIO PLAN :-   -: BENCH ELEVATION :-

2
The urban environment

With materials ready to hand and the studio in order, you are ready to tackle a design brief. If you live in or visit a town or city, you will find yourself surrounded by an enormous variety of manmade shapes and forms ideal for visual research and development. Choose any of the streets, buildings, urban objects or symbols, ruins, advertisements, the old or the new, whatever grabs your attention. Use this rich source of material for your original research, then develop your drawings and other visual images into experimental work and final realization of the project. Enjoy each stage for itself: *observation, research, experimentation* and finally the *realization* of your design.

Your brief is to research a particular locality within a self-defined boundary. This might include:

- walking round the locality and noting areas of interest to you

- taking a series of photographs of patterns, colours, forms, graphics or just shapes that come to your attention
- drawing a series of ten-minute sketches of particular items, for example, shopfronts, street furniture, doors
- taking a crayon rubbing of textures or patterns
- making a collection of cuttings from local magazines and newspapers
- making a study of a particular building, inside and out – find out all you can about its construction, history and usage

11 *Detail of slab-built construction with incised surface pattern*

12 *Spiral wedging*

13 *Cut and wedge*

- going to a high place after dark and drawing the skylines (cut them out of dark paper to show the silhouette)
- drawing a map of the area – analyse the different spaces and represent each one with a differently drawn texture
- carefully studying and recording a wall or pavement pattern
- observing and recording how groups of people interact with stairs and entrances in a variety of public buildings

References

Look at the work of the Chinese potters of the Han dynasty (see page 78), who built whole towers and temples of slabbed clay and assembled them unglazed. They also made kilns, pigsties and many other buildings which would have formed part of their urban environment.

Modern sources of inspiration might include the work of Bryan Newman who makes models of tower blocks, bridges and whole villages, influenced by the traditions of the ancient Chinese potters, and Ian Godfrey who builds cityscapes round the perimeters of his bowls.

The sixteenth-century Italian majolica painters used the urban scenes and fashions of the day to describe actual and mythical environments. In the same spirit, Eduardo Paolozzi has decorated the London Underground at Tottenham Court Road tube station with colourful mosaics, and much of his sculpture is composed of objects discarded by city-dwellers.

Wedging and clay preparation

You will probably be working with machine-prepared clay. Alternatively, instructions for preparing freshly dug clay are given on page 54. There are three basic reasons for preparing clay by hand, even if you have bought a fresh bag from the suppliers:

- to take out excess moisture – wedge very wet clay on an absorbent surface, such as clean plaster or smooth bricks
- to smooth out lumps – very lumpy clay might need 'weathering' by leaving it for a few days (longer if possible)
- to remove air bubbles – these could make the clay explode during the bisque firing (the air inside each bubble expands with heat)

You can prepare the clay by spiral kneading, Japanese-style (see page 20); alternatively, you can cut it with a wire into wedges, give each 'slice' a quarter-turn then bang it firmly down to knock out the air (see page 20). Both methods require practice under guidance. You can tell when the clay is ready by cutting it to see if there are any holes (air bubbles) left inside.

Making clay slabs

The photograph below shows the workbench with tools ready to make slabs of clay. On a clean, flat table, lay a smooth canvas or heavy linen cloth. Place two sticks, of the thickness you want the clay slabs, on the cloth with the prepared clay in the middle. These rolling guides are the best way to ensure the slabs are all the same thickness.

You will also need a rolling pin, a ruler, a clay knife, a damp sponge, modelling tools, rubber kidney, paint-brushes, a tub of clay slip or slurry, paper templates, a sketchbook or page of designs, a turntable and flat boards large enough to put the clay slabs between until they are leather-hard.

14 *Tools laid out for preparing slabs*

Begin by pressing the clay flat with the palms of your hands and leaning on it. This prevents the rolling pin from getting wet straight away, which would cause the clay to stick to it.

Roll out the clay, using short strokes and turning it over from time to time to keep the texture even. Allow space between the rolling guides for the clay to grow wider, and take care that the cloth does not wrinkle into folds.

When the clay is an even thickness, it is ready to be cut out, using a knife and ruler or a template. You may want to work directly with the wet clay slabs, or to dry them to leather-hard and then cut them out more accurately. Wet clay slabs are easily joined by pressing them together. Leather-hard slabs will need to be scored on the surfaces to be joined and pasted with thick slip or slurry paste; it helps to beat the joins firmly with a flat wooden stick to ensure their adhesion.

Making tiles

A clay tile is a flat slab of clay cut to size and shape. To make evenly sized tiles designed to fit together, you need to take exact measurements and to prepare each batch of clay at the same stage of wetness. Use a tile-cutter and a cardboard or wooden template on prepared, slightly stiff clay. Leave the tiles to dry on a clean, porous surface, such as wood, and cover them with another wooden board to ensure that they dry flat.

Tiles do not always have to be square. Complex geometric designs from Ancient Persia show what incredible mathematicians their craftsmen were. You could make a tile panel depicting an urban scene, with individual tiles in the shape of each building or object.

When the tiles are leather-hard, carefully cut out the shapes so that they will not distort. The maximum size of a single tile should be the width of the span of your hand. Where clay has built up on the surface, a corresponding amount must be hollowed from the back. This is because all parts of a ceramic piece must be the same thickness to ensure even firing.

Design brief

Research your chosen urban environment within a given locality. Construct some of your drawings in paper as paper sculptures, and reassess the proportions and shapes. You will then be ready to build a clay structure, using slabs of clay decorated with coloured slips.

After the period of time you have allotted, bring all your research materials together to decide how best they can be

Fig. 2 *Urban landscape, drawing by Darren Cundasamy*

Fig. 3 *Designs for slabbed facets of earthenware by Darren Cundasamy*

used. Designing at this stage could be called 'creative fiddle' – you need to try out a few ideas, criticize them, change them, find out what pleases you, what seems to fit, and what to put aside as unsuitable.

In Figs 2 and 3, the applied decoration was composed of tiny offcuts from the clay slab, which were applied by the 'score, slip and press' method used for slab pots. Other decorative lines were incised in the leather-hard clay, then after careful drying and biscuit-firing the structure was dipped in a transparent earthenware honey glaze (see page 87). The base of the structure was carefully wiped clean from glaze with a damp sponge. This is important because the glaze is expected to adhere to the clay surface, and it would do the same to the kiln shelves, permanently.

The structure is now prepared for the second glaze firing to a higher temperature, in this case earthenware, about 1080°C or cone 01.

During the firing process, the glaze powder melts to form a glassy surface, and the oxide colours in the slips and glazes are brought out.

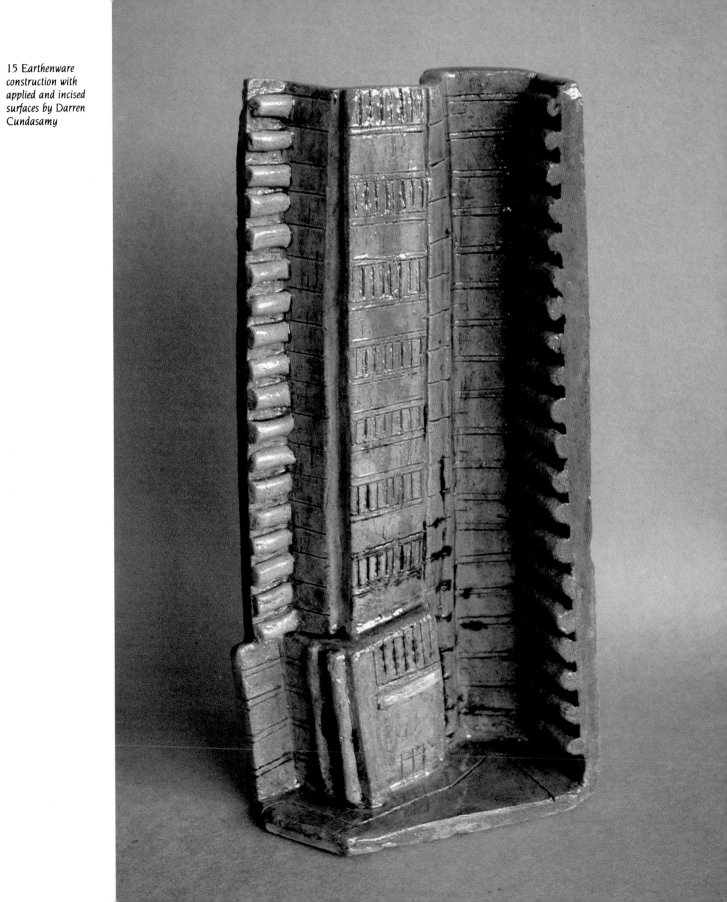

15 Earthenware construction with applied and incised surfaces by Darren Cundasamy

Slab pots

Prepare some slabs of clay with which to build a clay structure. Roll out enough clay for all the parts and apply any slip or impressed decoration while it is still flat. In Fig. 3, various coloured slips were applied using sponges, brushes, fingers, etc., and the clay was then left to become leather-hard before cutting.

Undo your paper sculpture and lay it on the clay to act as a template for the structure. Cut out all the pieces. You may have to recut some of the clay edges and mitre the corners to make the angles required to fit the sides together (see Fig. 5). Score both sides of the cut edges to be joined and apply a thick slurry of building slip. Press the slipped edges together firmly so that some of the slip oozes out.

Complete the structure and leave it until the shine has dried from the oozed slip, showing that it is stiffer. Using a round-ended modelling tool or the blunt end of a paint-brush, neaten the oozed slip to make a firm, smooth join.

Dry the structure slowly and evenly, checking carefully that none of the joins come apart. If they do while the clay is still leather-hard, apply more slip, otherwise you could repair a small split after the biscuit firing. Do not despair if the whole structure falls apart – you can rebuild it and practise scoring, slipping and joining the edges more thoroughly.

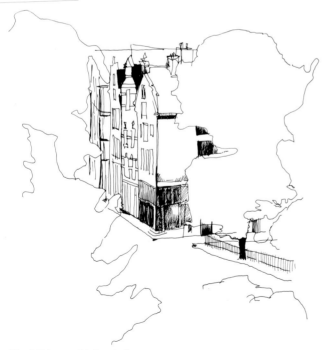

Fig. 4 Keizergracht, Amsterdam

The Temple of Light

This structure was designed to make use of an internal light source. After making drawings of windows and archways, the structure was developed from a series of pierced clay slabs (see Fig. 5), with an inner removable chamber and a seated dome.

First, a paper sculpture was made, life size plus 10 per cent to allow for shrinkage of the clay. It was important to be precise to allow for the size of the electric filament and to check that the method of assembly was possible.

Eight tiles for the walls, a top and a base were cut from leather-hard slabs of white earthenware body. A dome was coiled for the roof. The side edges of the eight wall tiles were mitred for neatness and to give more surface areas to bond the clay walls together.

The four tiles forming the inner chamber were decorated by cutting out diamond patterns while the clay was leather-hard; the larger slabs for the outer walls were cut with arched shapes. In each case, care was taken to leave an even amount of clay between the cut-outs so that the clay would dry evenly, otherwise cracks could be caused by the tension between wet and dry areas.

The four inner walls were joined and placed in the centre of the base. The inside of the base was marked and a low ridge built up inside that mark to make a register for the inner walls, which were not to be fixed in place. The four outer walls were joined together and fixed onto the base.

A round hole large enough for the inner walls to go through was cut in the top slab. A ridge was then made to make the seating holding the coiled, domed roof in place. The roof was also to be removable.

The parts were all assembled and carefully dried *in situ*, to discourage warping. When they were completely dry, the temple was biscuit-fired in its assembled position. There was no danger that the pieces would stick together as this requires the 'score, slip and press' method, but warping might still have been a problem if the separate parts of the temple had been fired apart.

After bisque firing, the three parts were dipped in a white majolica tin glaze to give maximum light reflection.

As the three parts were to be fired separately the second time, the base of the roof dome, inner walls and temple were carefully wiped free of glaze with a damp sponge, so the glaze would not fuse them together. They were then fired to earthenware temperature, as the glaze required.

After firing, the parts were assembled and an electric filament was fitted from the rear. It would also be possible to use a slow-burning candle or nightlight.

16 Earthenware construction from slip-dipped, trailed and combed slabs by David Cooper

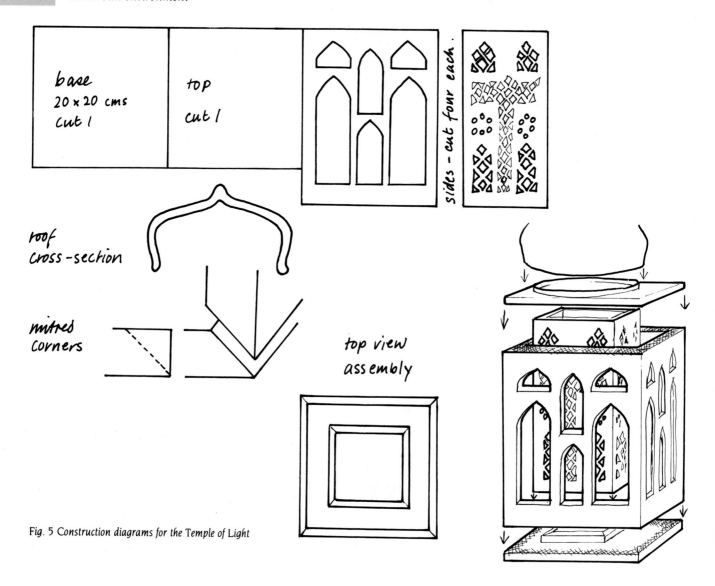

base
20 x 20 cms
cut 1

top
cut 1

sides – cut four each.

roof
cross-section

mitred
corners

top view
assembly

Fig. 5 Construction diagrams for the Temple of Light

sides - cut four each.

More ideas for urban environment projects

1 Press urban detritus onto soft clay to make an image of a house, street or city.

2 Choose a method of making lines in clay and draw directly on the clay surface.

3 Make a small, very detailed model of your favourite building or model a shopfront in great detail.

4 Draw the front of a local building of note. Slip-trail the design onto a tile, panel or large moulded dish.

5 Roll out a large slab of clay and loosely mark one of your drawings on it. When the clay is leather-hard, cut it out round the main forms like a jigsaw. Leave it unglazed.

6 As **5**, but glaze different parts with a variety of matt stoneware glazes to show depth.

7 Make a frieze of various buildings, using clay tiles cut in silhouette. Glaze them all in one dark, matt colour.

8 Make a slab bridge for a model railway.

9 Make a model church to hold a nightlight, which would shine through the cut-out windows.

10 Design a futuristic environment. Make an overall plan and then a complete section, like an architect's model.

11 Design and make a detailed scale model of the house you would like to live in.

12 Make a large tile showing the exterior façade of a shop selling ceramics.

13 Make a tile with a ceramic frame that acts as a 'picture window' for a view of a cityscape.

14 Create an imaginary environment of symbolic objects.

Other suggestions for related themes might include buildings, doorways, interiors, cars, transport lorries, street furniture, market stalls, neon lights, steps and stairs, and wallcoverings.

3
Landscape and natural forms

The countryside is a rich source of visual material waiting for use, directly or indirectly. The research for this brief includes looking at all things which are not manmade, from naturally occurring landforms to cultivated fruit and vegetables.

Study the early work of Michael Casson, who was influenced by the landscape near his home, or Victor Margrie's series of porcelain 'sky bowls'. Look at the work of Ewen Henderson, whose watercolour landscapes have informed his marvellously textured and coloured asymmetrical coil pots. Portuguese country potters produce an incredible range of tableware based on cabbages, and English seaside shops sell all manner of designs related to shells (see the teapot on page 72).

Your research will probably take you to the marvellous work of potteries like Royal Doulton in Lambeth, which designed in the style of Art Nouveau. This fashion, at its height in the 1920s in Europe, was based on drawings of prints and flowers, and was inspired by William Morris and the Arts and Crafts Movement.

On the other side of the world, Nigerian potters in the village of Kwali incise linear motifs representing local flora and fauna on the sides of their large waterpots. And Roman potters in fifth-century Britain made small thrown pots shaped like the seedheads of poppies.

18 *Detail of a hand-painted landscape from a modern Chinese earthenware planter*. Private collection

Research

Natural forms

1   Take a nature walk and pick up as many different types of leaves, pebbles and nuts as possible.

2   In autumn, press fallen leaves between blotting paper and keep them in a book.

3   Find an orchard and draw as many different shapes and forms of apple that you can find.

4   Make a large drawing of a nut in its shell.

5   Cut a cabbage in half and make a line drawing of the leaf patterns.

6   In autumn, draw as many varieties of mushroom as you can find.

7   Collect gourd-type fruits (squash, melon, pumpkin, etc.) and dry them out thoroughly in the sun or a slow oven.

8   Carefully draw a globe artichoke.

9   Draw some dried gourds or a Caribbean calabash.

10   Look at some plant sections through a microscope, then draw them with a fine felt pen.

Landscape

1   Make linear drawings of the patterns made by ploughed fields seen from a distance.

2   Take a series of photographs of bare landscapes with rolling hills.

3   Express **1** and **2** as very simple line drawings.

4   Tear long strips of newsprint and paste them down to indicate a landscape.

5   Experiment with variations of **4**, using different papers.

6   Using watercolours, paint the sky in as many different moods as possible.

7   Make a pen-and-ink line drawing of a clump of trees on top of a hill.

8   Draw a hedgerow, using as many different drawing techniques as you know to describe its textures.

9   Simply look at landscapes.

Fig. 6 *Beach pebbles with striations, Llantwit Major, Wales*

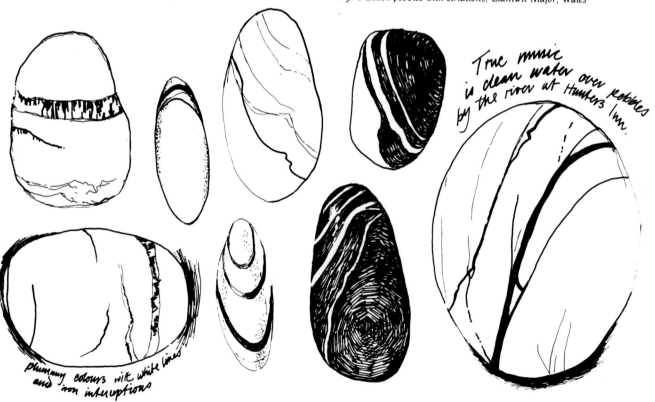

Other themes

Develop your own research into other areas, for example, trees, the river bank, the beach, fruit, buds, mountains, the forest, animals or vegetables.

19 Pinch-pot 'pebbles' made with a variety of different clays, showing a range of decorative techniques, by the author

Pinch pots

Pinch pots can be made from any type of clay body. They are often used to test the plasticity of clay, or to gauge the firing temperature of a found clay body. The name is derived from the method of making; because you shape the pot from the inside with your thumb, they are also known as 'thumb pots'.

Step 1   Take a piece of wedged clay about the size of a tennis ball. Pat and roll it between your hands to make it as perfectly round as possible. Prepare another ball the same way.

Step 2   Stick your thumb in one of the clay spheres, as near to and as deeply in the middle as you can judge.

Step 3   Keeping your thumb in the middle, use your fingers to pinch the clay wall evenly round until it opens up in the form of an upright bowl. Continue until the clay wall is as thin as your little finger. To make an enclosed form, leave this bowl standing on its rim while you use the other clay sphere to make another bowl, with the same-sized rim.

Step 4   Moisten the lips of the two bowls and join them together, trapping an air bubble inside. This will be easy to do if the bowls have even rims; if the rims have become uneven during the pinching process, cut them straight with a clay knife before you join them.

Step 5   Gently roll, shape or beat the small hollow ball into a cohesive form, using the trapped air bubble for support. Be careful not to compress the clay so much that the air escapes.

Step 6   When the form is leather-hard, you can decorate it and cut a small airhole to allow for safe drying and firing.

Decorating pebble pots

Plate 20 shows a collection of small hollow forms based on the drawings of pebbles shown in Fig. 6. Each uses a different clay and explores a variety of surface treatments and cultural references.

1   Textured, white, stoneware 'T' material, inlaid with terracotta and scraped all over to reveal the textured body. The whiteness reminded me of dried bones and the red slip of blood feeding them with nutrients.

2   A sticky yellow clay sample from a hole in the road, incised and biscuit-fired to terracotta brick red. This was a test to see whether I really had spotted clay being dug up where a pipe was being laid in a deep hole in a city street.

20 *Pinch pots in progress, with source materials*

3 A sandy grey body, incised and part-burnished, and fired in a garden bonfire. I was thinking about nuts – almonds, walnuts, plum, date and cherry stones – how they dry and split along hidden joints.

4 A smooth grey stoneware body, inlaid with different-coloured slips, burnished and fired unglazed to 1250°C. I had just seen an exhibition of indigenous Australian slip-painted, unglazed ware which had the same timeless quality as the river pebbles.

5 Reclaimed clay with added coarse fireclay, bisque-fired and dabbed all over with a variety of stoneware glazes. This was my 'conservation pot', using up all my small remnants of clay and glaze colours, making something permanent out of nothing and saving waste materials.

Landscape dishes

Large dishes give an excellent 'canvas' to explore the wider views and perspectives of a seascape or landscape. Your research drawings and observations should encourage you to think on a larger scale for this theme.

Technique

There are several ways to make a large flat dish and the method might be dictated by the decorative techniques you decide to employ. As ever, you would be advised to make a small maquette and to take it through the firing processes of bisque and glaze to check that the colours and textures will be suitable for your design.

The clay you use should be finely or coarsely textured with sand, grog or fireclay to reduce the risk of it cracking in the firing. Search through your supplier's catalogue for a St Thomas or raku body. Alternatively, use a familiar smooth body but wedge lots of sand into it until you can see a good texture when you cut the clay with a wire.

Method 1   Roll out a large slab of clay on a cloth, using rolling guides about 0.5 cm thick. Carefully lift the clay slab, either over your arm or still sticking to the cloth, and place it in a concave plaster mould. Using a damp natural sponge, ease the clay into every part of the mould taking care not to stretch or crack the rather 'short' body. Trim the edge of the clay with a cheese wire or clay harp.

When the clay is leather-hard, remove it from the mould and sponge the rim free of any potentially sharp edges.

Method 2   Roll out the clay slab on a weave-patterned cloth or piece of rough sacking. Place it over a convex form to go

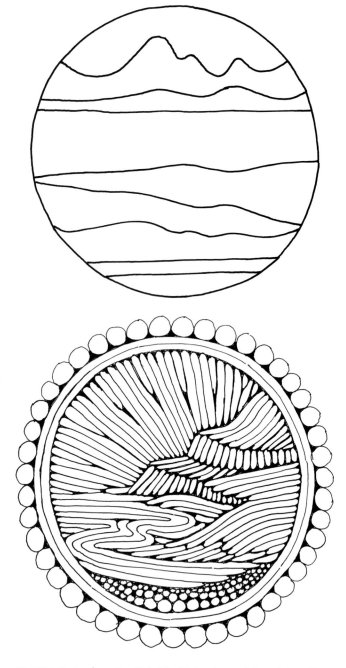

Fig. 7(a) *Design for a stencilled dish.* (b) *Landscape dish made by coiling method 3 (the reverse is smooth, with an applied foot ring)*

leather-hard; use a convex plaster mushroom-shaped mould, a bisque-fired dish or a clay mound covered with cloth.

34

21 Press-moulded stoneware dish, using applied and incised decoration, by
Sotis Filippides

Method 3   Prepare a quantity of clay coils, either by hand or in a wad box (see page 45). Coil a landscape design over a mushroom mould, then smooth the design away with a stiff rubber kidney. Fix an even coil of clay on top of the clay hump and model it in so that it will form a foot when the dish is reversed. When the form is leather-hard, take it off the mould and your design will be visible again inside (see Fig. 7b).

Method 4   Turn a kitchen stool upside down. Tie the four corners of a piece of linen or canvas cloth to the upturned legs, creating a shallow dip in the cloth. Roll out the clay for the dish and cut the edges to form the shape of the finished design, using a paper template if necessary. Carefully place the cut form on the cloth to turn leather-hard.

Method 5   Roll out the clay slab and cut it to shape, using a paper template. Turn up the edges and place a fat coil of clay underneath until the dish is leather-hard. Remove the coil and fettle (smooth) the edge of the flat dish.

Slip-stencilled decoration

A large dish made in a plaster mould (see Method I above) can be decorated with a slip-stencilled landscape.

Roll out the clay and fit it in the mould, as described. Wipe the surface of the clay until it is smooth, even and damp. Now tear strips of newsprint the length of the mould and lay them on the damp clay surface. Press them in place with a sponge so that all the paper sticks to the clay. Pour slip into the dish and swirl it round till it evenly covers both clay and newsprint. Pour out the excess slip and leave the dish just until the shine dries from the surface. Carefully peel away the paper to show your design.

Repeat the paper-and-slip process with other coloured slips until the design is complete. Biscuit-fire and glaze with a clear earthenware glaze.

Coiled landscape pot

A tall coil pot could use the Scottish landscape as a starting point, reflecting the natural colours of lichen-covered rocks, stone walls, dykes, lochs, skies and mountains.

Assemble a variety of clays of differing texture and colour. You could add body stains to some, or keep to natural greys, white and terracotta. You might need to make some test samples to see which clays join together easily, as differing compositions might cause some difficulty. If this happens, wedge together a little of the incompatible body with fine or coarse grog until the test is successful.

Ewen Henderson often joins bodies as diverse as porcelain and crank to create a rich, uneven surface texture (see Plate 22). He has exhibited his watercolour landscapes with his clay constructions, identifying the source of his exciting colours and organic forms.

Having decided on the bodies to use, assemble the pot by pressing them out in uneven strips. Cut out a circular or oval base, then start to build up the sides, using one of the strips of clay bent round to form a shallow cylinder. Join the wall to the base by modelling the two surfaces together on the inside and the outside, until the hairline crack between them is invisible. Continue to build up the wall in this way, using alternating colours and textures. Pay particular attention to joining the strips together inside and out, and stop to let the pot stiffen if the walls appear unsafe.

Protect the top edge of the pot from drying out by covering it with a damp cloth until you are ready to continue building. When the form is completed, it can be confirmed or modified by gently knocking or beating it with a flat stick. This compresses the clay and stabilizes the construction. The leather-hard form can be decorated with surface treatment, scraping it down with a metal kidney to bring out the rougher, sandy textures, or burnishing it with the back of a spoon to make it smooth.

Dry the pot and bisque-fire. You could glaze the inside of the pot if you wanted to make it non-porous and therefore more functional. Alternatively, you could fire it to a higher temperature without a glaze to bring out the natural body colours.

22 Part of a series called 'Leaning and Thrusting' by Ewen Henderson. Bone china and porcelain laminated onto a stoneware core, the colour and surface pattern arising from the making. Private collection

Impressed decoration

Fig. 8 Design for a tile with impressed decoration, using grasses

Make a permanent record of grasses, seeds and flowers collected from a particular place at a particular time of year by taking their impressions on the smooth surface of rolled-out clay. Test which grasses leave the best design and decide whether to make small medallions, individual tiles or a set of tiles showing a complete landscape design.

Use a stoneware body. If it is textured, burnish the leather-hard surface of the tiles with the back of a spoon until it is glossy. Then bisque-fire the tiles.

Mix equal quantities of iron and copper oxides (a pinch of each for one tile) with enough water to make a thin wash. Paint this thinly over the impressed clay surface so that the water carries the oxide grains into the floral designs like a shadow. Sponge away any oxide that is too thick and dark for your liking. Brush off any unwanted paintbrush lines with a dry brush, and leave the tiles to dry.

Fire the tiles to a stoneware temperature without further glazing. The oxides will give a sheen to the design, creating an antique effect.

You could experiment with tiny flowerheads impressed into porcelain to make jewellery using this method of oxide decoration.

23 Coil-built vine fruit polished with firegrate blacking, silver wire attached to form the tendril, by Rydal Bowtell

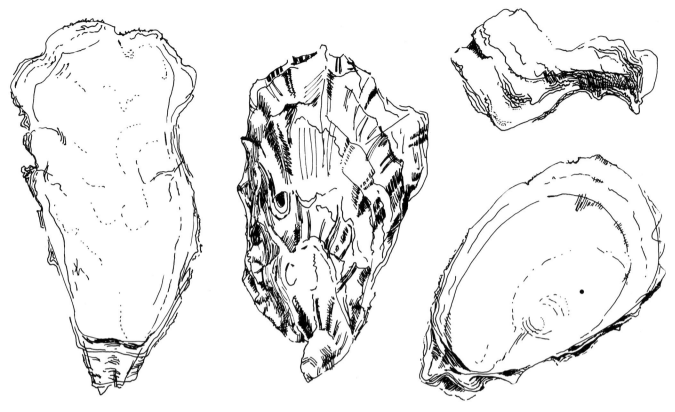

Other suggestions for projects

1   Press *objets trouvés* from a country walk onto soft clay surfaces to form a landscape, tree, flower, etc.

2   As **1**, then wrap the clay round a cardboard tube to make a cylindrical vase.

3   As **1**, but on a very large scale which can be cut up when leather-hard to make a wall panel.

4   Make a landscape using slip-trailed decoration.

5   Look at Thomas Toft's seventeenth-century plates, then slip-trail your own tree.

6   Make a soup tureen in the shape of a bundle of leeks for serving leek soup, a cabbage dish, etc.

7   Coil a bowl with different colours and textures of clay to represent a landscape of rolling hills.

Fig. 9 Oyster shells used as designs for bottles

8   Make a large coil pot based on the shape and form of a single peanut.

9   Make a paper sculpture, using secondary source material such as a picture or photograph. Use this template to make a slab pot which you can then decorate and glaze in your own way.

10   Press a slab of clay over the collage of a landscape so that the design is pressed onto the clay surface. Carefully lift off the clay and leave it to dry in a mould.

11   Make a plate in a plaster mould, using the untrimmed or cut edge as part of the design.

12   Make a strip-built bottle based on the shell drawings in Fig. 9.

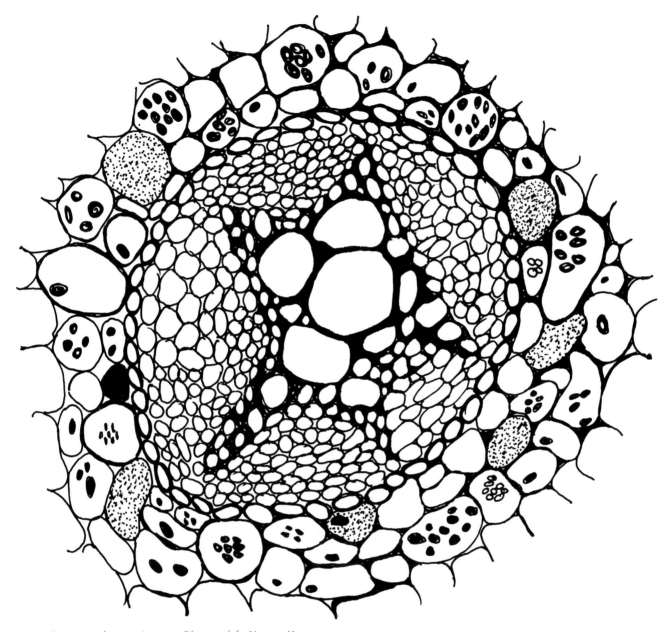

Fig. 10 *Plant section from a microscope. Photograph by Norman Unger*

4
Faces and figures

The human face and figure have always inspired artists and craftspeople, from the earliest cave paintings in different-coloured minerals to the present day. For example, American ceramic artist and humourist Robert Arneson incorporates a self-portrait in just about everything he does. In sixteenth-century Florence portraits of fashionable ladies were painted on circular plates with elaborate painted borders.

In the past, painted portraits and busts fulfilled some of the functions of portrait photography today. Each medium still has its own part to play but the sheer power of physical presence created in a three-dimensional ceramic form contributes to its expressive potential.

Some of the earliest figurative sculptures were tiny votive figures found in Egyptian tombs. At the other end of the scale, there is the huge Chinese army of tomb guardians (see page 77), where hundreds of figures and horses were made slightly larger than life size, probably to frighten off tomb-robbers and escort the dead into another life.

Research

1 Draw self-portraits in the mirror in a variety of media.

2 Photograph a friend's head from every angle.

3 Fill a sketchbook with life drawings.

4 Collect cut-outs of sporting figures from magazines and newspapers.

5 Make detailed studies of your other hand and your feet.

6 Draw a skeleton to check the proportions of a figure.

7 Research the names and shapes of the body's muscle groups.

8 In the park or from a window, draw people walking past as quickly as you can, noting the shapes they make together.

9 Visit a museum and draw in detail any plaster or bronze figures that you find there.

10 Draw your clothes hanging up, remembering the form of the figure inside.

11 Go to a sports match solely for the purpose of drawing the players in action

12 Sketch people reading in the local library.

13 Make a colour study of somebody working in the kitchen.

14 Make a series of maquettes showing the variety of activities you see people doing around you, for example, sitting, standing, leaning, resting, working.

15 Study the latest hairstyles and practise ways of painting hair using watercolours. Use these to analyse how you would model hair in clay.

16 Research different methods of coiling by visiting potters' studios and watching demonstrations.

24 Detail of thrown and hand-painted nineteenth-century porcelain plate depicting courtly Japanese women. Private collection

Coil pots

This method of building pots is one of the oldest we know. Many museums have examples dating back to the twentieth century BC from Mesopotamia, Egypt, Crete and India. Coiling is still a reliable way of constructing larger forms, easy to learn initially but requiring great skill to perfect.

The indigenous population of Central and South America make painted slip-decorated bowls and jars, by the traditional coiled technique. African potters, mainly women, make huge, perfectly round waterpots; they store their grain in hut-sized granaries constructed with mud and straw coils.

The skill of these potters is admired and emulated today in making non-functional, sculptural designs.

Coiling the form of a torso

Make a maquette, then decide on the size of the finished piece and calculate the dimensions of the base.

You have a choice of ways to make the base. You can cut it from a slab of clay; you can coil it from the centre, then smooth it over; or you can dispense with a base altogether and begin with one coil, making a ring the size and shape required.

Coils are formed from a 'sausage' of clay taken from a prepared lump of soft, plastic clay. The sausage can be evened out and elongated by rolling it between both hands, in the manner of the Nigerian women potters, or rolling it on a porous wooden tabletop. Use both hands to make as even a coil as possible, about the thickness of your little finger. Another method of making coils is to press the prepared clay through an extruder or wad box.

If you have cut out the base, start by pressing a row of coils around the edge, flattening each coil as you go with your thumb. Work as evenly and rhythmically as you can to make a consistently thin clay wall. The coil winds round and round, up the side of the pot (see Plate 25).

Every three or four rows of coils, stop and smudge the inside together to make a smooth surface with no visible joins. The outside can be treated the same way, unless you want the pattern of the coil-building to be part of the decoration.

If you want the form to grow wider, place new coils on the outer edge of the previous ones; if you want the form to grow narrower, place them on the inner edge.

When the structure is complete, lightly beat out any uneven surfaces with a smooth, flat wooden stick.

After the form has stiffened to leather-hard, scrape the surface with a metal kidney to define the form and raise the surface texture of the clay. If you want a smoother surface, burnish the clay with the back of a dessertspoon.

Some potters like to coil with fat coils and mould them onto the form with their thumb in one process. It is also possible to roll the coil, pinch it into a triangular formation and then apply this to the top of the clay wall, modelling inside and outside at the same time. You could also coil with a cut-out flat strip like a shallow slab pot. Try different methods to see what suits you.

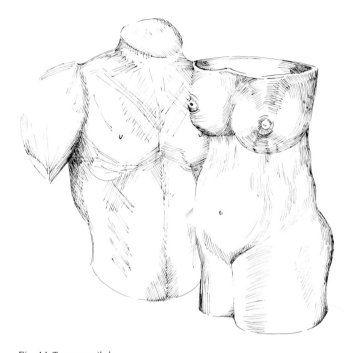

Fig. 11 *Torsoes, coiled*

25 A *coil pot in progress*

Portraits

Plate 26 shows a simply constructed coil pot made by Jacob Sutton to portray his wife and child. Cobalt oxide was mixed with water and thinly painted on top of a white majolica earthenware glaze immediately before firing.

Fig. 12 Images from the Pitt Rivers Museum, Oxford. (Left) Painted wooden shield, probably Papuan Gulf. (Centre) Mask of painted cloth on a cane framework, surmounted by a ball of burrs and with a nose of brown paper, Witu Island, Melanesia. (Right) Ceremonial shield for hanging in temples, over 100 years old, Motu Motu, New Guinea

26 Family portrait by Jacob Sutton. Artist's collection

Masks from many countries of the world can be invaluable sources of design for a more interpretative approach to portraiture (see Fig. 12).

a puff ball of fibres

Moulded portraits

Plate 28 shows a self-portrait by student Jameson Davis in celebration of a new haircut, made using a two-piece plaster press mould. This type of mould was produced to facilitate experimentation with glazes and surfaces on a similar form. It can often be divided from ear to ear, but this profile division is an alternative strategy.

The portrait was first modelled using a solid block of clay, taking care that there would be no undercuts as these would prevent the two moulds lifting cleanly away from the form, and would scrape away a modelled protuberance. The nostrils therefore had to be filled in and opened at a later stage, and the ears were modelled pressed flat to the sides of the head.

Preparing the completed model for the right-hand mould meant laying it on one side, taking care that the profile was parallel to the table surface. A flat board was placed at the back of the head and a strip of linoleum was bent round the structure about 4 cm (1½ in) away from the form (see Fig. 13), held in place with string and coils of clay.

A platform of clay was then built round the profile, firm enough to support the wet plaster for the few minutes until it set. A mark was made on the lino wall 4 cm (1½ in) above the highest point of the clay form. This was to indicate the depth of plaster to be used, so that the completed mould would be roughly the same thickness throughout and would therefore dry the pressed clay form more evenly.

Plaster of Paris was mixed in a flexible basin, using the empirical method, as follows. Visually judge how much plaster might be required, and fill a basin with about one third of that amount of water. Sprinkle the plaster on the water as evenly as possible, without stirring it. The powder will sink into the water, absorbing it. When it begins to form peaks on the surface, stir it quickly and briefly with one hand to make sure there are no lumps.

Before the plaster starts to feel warm and to set, pour it into the prepared mould. Check for leaks and plug with soft clay if necessary. If the plaster level does not reach the mark, you will need to disturb the plaster surface and to add a fresh bowl of plaster. Leave the plaster to set. It should feel quite warm as heat is given off as a by-product of the chemical change taking place.

When the plaster is completely set, take apart the wood and lino structure and turn the plaster upside down, with the clay model still in place. Make several indentations in the horizontal plaster surface with a small coin. These will act to locate the second mould when it is in use.

Take a thick solution of soapy water or washing-up liquid and paint over the plaster surface to prevent the new plaster sticking to it.

Replace the wooden board and the lino, marking the height for the plaster. Make the second half of the mould in

the same way. After setting, carefully open the two halves and take out the solid clay model, which can now be discarded. Dry the plaster forms thoroughly before use.

Roll out two slabs of clay and ease them into the plaster moulds with a damp sponge to ensure an accurate fit. Cut off the excess clay with a wire, and sponge or slip where the clay edges will join. Press the two moulds together firmly and leave them until the clay inside starts to shrink away from the plaster.

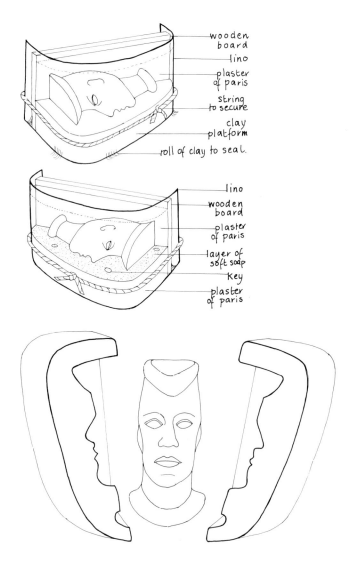

Fig. 13 *Making a two-piece face mould*

Fig. 14 Bellarmines, sixteenth-century German salt-glazed wine jars with sprigged portraits said to represent Cardinal Bellarmine

Carefully open the moulds to find the completed portrait inside. Tidy, or fettle, the joined surfaces with a modelling tool and damp sponge.

At this leather-hard stage the portrait is open to minor changes. You could open up the nostrils, pierce the eye pupils to give an appearance of sight, make any clay additions or paint it with coloured slips.

Dry, bisque-fire and glaze in the normal way.

More ideas for portraits

1   Draw a friend, then slip-trail a simplified design of the portrait on a moulded dish. Slip-trail an edging pattern to act as a frame.

2   Make a set of tiles and slip-trail a figure across the whole panel.

3   Make a portrait of a friend using a coiling structure.

4   Mould a dish and slip-paint a figure study from life for the decoration.

5   Model an unclothed figure directly from life in terra-cotta.

6   Coil a flower pot in the shape of a face, to house a trailing plant which would represent the hair.

7   Paint a portrait in oxides on top of a white glazed plate.

8   Make a series of maquettes of sporting figures in active poses.

9   Make a model of someone doing a job, including the tools and equipment to make a complete tableau.

10   Coil the head and shoulders of someone reading.

11   Model a group of figures who make an interesting shape together.

12   From the drawing of a mask, make a paper construction which then becomes a template for a slab-built pot.

13   From an illustration, make as exact a copy as you can of an ancient Greek sculpture.

14   Make a plainly formed pot and as you are building it draw a face or figure into the surface with coils.

28 Self-portrait by Jameson Davis. Author's collection

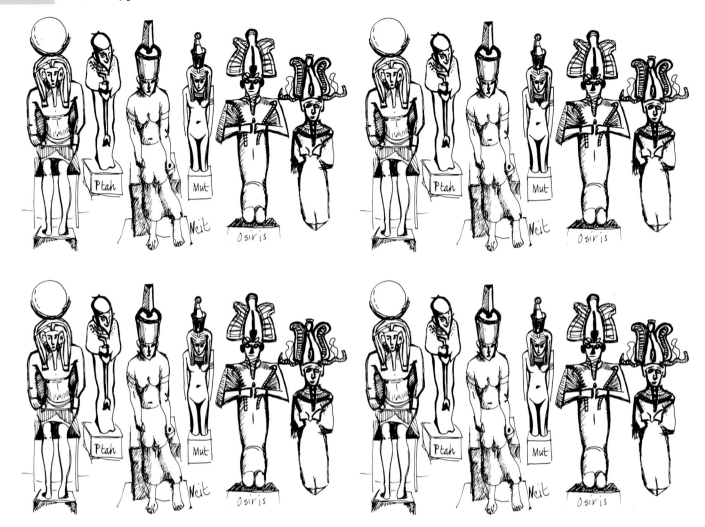

Fig. 15 Frieze of miniature Egyptian gods

29 Group of unglazed figures in the form of a whistle, moulded, modelled, burnished and slip-painted by hand, Ayacucho, Peru. Picture courtesy of Oxfam

5
Portfolio of tests

You should now be ready to clarify the range of surfaces and colours available to you within your particular studio setting. In any craft there is a range of possibilities to explore, and also limitations.

I am going to assume that you have access to an electrically fired kiln, which normally fires to an 'oxidizing atmosphere'. Fire needs oxygen to continue to burn brightly, where oxygen is freely available, and this is known as an oxidizing atmosphere. All kilns fire with either this atmosphere or an 'oxygen-reduced' atmosphere, but for reduction you would need to have a wood-, oil- or gas-fired kiln. This involves introducing a material into the kiln when it has reached temperature in order to 'reduce' the oxygen availability, altering the usual oxide colours.

If you are working in an established pottery or attending a class, you may have a marvellous range of tests and experiments available for you to see, touch and examine. If not, or if you want to have your own reference material, the following suggested experiments may be useful.

Most ceramic materials suppliers will provide 'starter pack' samples of bodies, colours and glazes, which are ideal for building up a portfolio. If they provide colour illustrations, remember that your own facilities may produce very different shades. There is really no substitute for your own tests.

You will need to decide how you want to store or display finished tests. This chapter gives some ideas but you may think of others. You could make thin, flat tiles to mount on card and store in a drawer or portfolio, or a series of shallow bowls with holes in their centres, screwed onto a wooden display board. You could also hang tests from the rims of your glaze or slip buckets for instant reference.

Keep careful notes about your tests so that you can reproduce the successful ones. If you are doing a series of experiments on maquettes or thrown shapes, make an outline drawing of each one in a notebook, with notes and comments as the work progresses.

Preparing and testing freshly dug clay

You will probably have to rely on local knowledge to find where the clay is in your neighbourhood. If you live near a river, look for a place where the earth, instead of being dark and crumbly, is yellow and sticky.

Take a handful of freshly dug clay and pick it over morsel by morsel, taking out any tiny stones, leaves or other organic matter.

Make a small pinch pot by putting your thumb into the middle of the ball of clay, squeezing the clay in a pinching movement until it is about the thickness of your little finger. Leave the pot to dry out thoroughly, then fire to about 750°C. You could take precautions against ruining another kiln bat by firing the pot inside a larger stoneware bisque bowl.

After firing, examine the pinch pot. If it looks like the rest of your earthenware bisque, you have found a source of clay which you can use for larger pieces. Try testing it at higher temperatures to find its maximum tolerance.

If the little bowl has sagged a bit, you might still have a useful source of earthenware slip. Reinforce the body with grog or fireclay and try firing it again. If the pot has melted and bubbled, the clay is not going to be useful material at all. If bits of the pot have exploded, you did not clean it well enough and it may contain some pieces of flint. Document each find with its source.

To prepare larger quantities of freshly dug clay

You can pick over the clay as above, which will get rid of most impurities, and wedging could find the rest. This is a gentle therapeutic activity, especially outdoors.

A more certain way to get rid of the impurities would be to do on a small scale what clay manufacturers do with mechanical help. Dry out the clay and break up larger lumps with a mallet. Place the clay in a bucket of water to slake overnight, then stir it until it becomes a thick slip.

Sieve the slip through a coarse sieve to take out stones, etc., then through a 60- or 80-mesh sieve, depending how fine you would like the body to be.

Leave the smooth slip to settle in a bucket and pour away the water that remains on the top. As the remaining water evaporates, the slip will become thicker and thicker until you can scoop it out and wedge it on a porous surface. It will now resemble the familiar 'plastic' state and this plasticity improves with keeping, even for a few days.

To compare the natural colours of different-fired clay bodies

Find as wide a variety of clay bodies as are available to you in the studio. Alternatively, use a sample pack of different clays from your supplier. I suggest at least an earthenware body, a raku body, a stoneware body and a porcelain. Decide how to store or display the results; I have used square, flat tiles (see Plate 31).

30 Tests showing fired surfaces treated with non-ceramic materials, including coloured waxes, oil-based paints and polishes

Make four of each sample. Dry and bisque-fire two of each sample. Dry and earthenware-fire one of each sample. Dry and stoneware-fire one of each sample.

Dip one bisque-fired earthenware and one raku body sample in a clear earthenware glaze and fire them to earthenware temperature (around 1080°C, cone 1). Dip one bisque-fired stoneware and one porcelain body sample in a clear stoneware glaze and fire them to stoneware temperature (around 1250°C, cone 8).

When all the firings are complete, mount the tests together and compare their natural colours. Note how the brown earthenware body in Plate 31 has bubbled at stoneware, which is clearly above its vitrification temperature.

To test clay shrinkage

All clay bodies shrink between the process of making, when the clay is in its plastic state, through to bisque-firing and the final glaze. Shrinkage will depend on the water content of the clay and the presence of refractory materials such as grog. You will find that different clays shrink up to 10 per cent.

You might need to test a clay for shrinkage if:

- you are trying out a clay recipe of your own
- it is a new clay on special offer at your suppliers
- someone else has given it to you to try
- you have just dug it up from the ground
- a finished piece must have an exact measurement

To make a collection of shrinkage tests, use a tile-cutter of fixed dimension or cut out a template of, say, 10 × 10 cm (4 × 4 in). You could use this template again when you have other clays to test.

Collect together different clay samples in a plastic state. Roll them out on cloth to a measured thickness, using rolling guides. Cut out the samples, using the template or a cutter. Remember to fettle the edges to prevent the hazard of sharp bits after firing, and mark each one with an identifying code. Note the code numbers in your record book. Leave them to dry slowly between boards to ensure flatness.

Fire each tile to its recommended temperature, following the manufacturer's catalogue, or the normal studio firing temperature, or your own guesswork. Measure each sample carefully and note it in your record book.

Different ways to make a line in clay

These experiments will give you a vocabulary of lines with which to carry out the surface decoration for many of the projects described in this workbook.

Roll out a smooth, fine-textured piece of clay on a cloth, using a rolling pin. Carefully smooth the clay surface with a rubber kidney for this surface will become your canvas.

If you draw a line in clay with a sharp point, the clay will simply push itself into two ridges. After biscuit-firing, these would be hard and sharp, particularly for the person unpacking the kiln, and you would need to flatten them with a rolling pin or flat tool. Experiment with other ways of drawing lines:

Fig. 16 *Set of textured tiles, Wimereux, France*

1   Press lines into the clay with the edge of a ruler, a piece of string or the curve of a lid.

2   When you have run out of things to impress, sponge the clay moist and apply what clay shapes you can on the remaining surface – a coil of clay, a contrasting-coloured coil of clay, a thin strip or ribbon of clay, a slip-trailed line, a row of dots or painted slip.

3   After the work has dried to leather-hard, you can make other lines. Try incising or cutting a line without leaving ridges. Incise shallow and wide lines.

While the clay is still leather-hard, fill some of the lines with a contrasting-coloured coil of soft clay or slip. When this has stiffened, scrape over the top with a metal kidney to level both coloured surfaces for a professional-looking 'inlay'.

After drying thoroughly and bisque-firing, other incised lines could be filled with contrasting-coloured or textured glaze.

31 *Tests for natural clay colours*

Decorative methods using coloured slips or engobes

Slip or engobe is a mixture of clay, water and colouring oxides sieved to a thick, creamy consistency. In its toughest, unsieved form, it is a slurry paste useful for joining slabs of clay together at the leather-hard stage. In its most refined form, it becomes *terra sigillata*, sieved through a 200-mesh sieve to a resultant fine texture which will burnish to a high polish without glazing.

Dipping

Slip is not a solution but a mixture which must be used quickly or it will separate. Decide how much or how little of the pot is to be dipped. When the pot is leather-hard and the slip just stirred, dip it briefly into the creamy mixture and shake off any drips. The pot will gradually soften as it absorbs the water from the slip, so leave it undisturbed until it reverts again to a leather-hard state.

Masking or stencilling

Instead of just dipping the clay form, you can mask off some areas with paper.

Cut or tear newsprint to use as a stencil. When the clay form is leather-hard, sponge the newsprint carefully onto the surface. Dip the masked pot into the slip, shake off the excess then leave it until it is leather-hard again.

As the slip dries, the edge of the paper stencil will become defined, making it easy to carefully peel it away to reveal your design. Dry the form, glaze and fire it in the normal way.

Sgraffito

This is the process of scratching away the soft layer of dipped slip in lines or areas, to reveal the contrasting colour of the clay beneath (see page 60).

Burnishing

This produces a glossy clay surface without glaze. It is best used on a fine clay surface, for which you might use a *terra sigillata* or fine coloured engobe.

After the dipped pot has returned to its leather-hard state, dry it still more until it is almost starting to dry out – at this stage you will get the brightest shine. Polish the surface of the form with the back of a metal spoon.

32 *A vocabulary of lines on clay*

Slip-trailing

In this method of decoration, the thick, creamy slip is piped through a rubber bulb or slip-trailer in the manner of icing a cake. Experiment initially on leather-hard clay until you can confidently trail an even line. Before you start, expel all the air from the slip-trailer – shake it so that the air rises to the surface, then gently squeeze it out. If you make any errors or unwanted blobs on the leather-hard surface, you can easily sponge them off.

Trailing on a wet ground

Choose a horizontal surface – tiles, a plate in a mould or pre-cut slabs. While the clay is still plastic, cover it with an even layer of slip and trail a contrasting slip onto the wet surface. Work quickly in as spontaneous a way as possible. When you have finished, lightly tap the mould or wooden board to flatten the slip-covered surface.

Marbling

Prepare as above with a variety of trailed slip colours in a simple design of lines or blobs. Instead of tapping the mould or board, agitate it with a quick circular motion until the slip colours begin to swirl into each other.

Feathering

Trail contrasting slip on a wet ground. Take a single bristle from a broom or a pin and drag thin strands of one colour into another. The effect should be like the decoration on top of a Battenburg cake.

Slip-painting

Use a variety of shaped Japanese brushes to exploit the calligraphic patterns made uniquely by each one. Although the painted slip will be opaque after firing, about half its volume will be lost in the drying, so paint thickly. Let one layer stiffen before adding another to keep the colours fresh. You will get a different range of hues after bisque, earthenware or stoneware firing, with or without transparent glazes.

Sponging

Instead of applying the slip to the leather-hard surface, try sponging it on in texture layers. Use a natural sponge or pieces of cut foam, trimmed with scissors to a variety of shapes – diamonds, circles, leaf motifs, etc.

Try a collage of different techniques, for example dip and burnish, marble and feather, stencil and sponge.

Sgraffito

This versatile method of decoration, originally Italian, consists of scratching through one surface to reveal another. Sgraffito is often most effective where a linear quality is required for decoration, or where a patch of foreground or background colour needs clear definition. Traditional Greek figured pots are a good example, mainly using red and black slips with the addition of some painted lines. American potter John Glick uses different layers of glaze or slip scratched through in an abstract design, using a hand-carved wooden comb or form to make the close parallel lines.

Tools for sgraffito can be anything that is comfortable to hold and has a point to draw with. Collect together a variety of tools: a pen nib, a piece of carved bamboo, a fork, a pointed lollipop stick, a dentist's pick, a plastic cocktail stick, etc.

Now make a series of tests on irregularly shaped pieces of clay to contrast the precision possible with sgraffito using different materials:

- terracotta clay covered with a layer of white slip, scratched through when it is leather-hard (taking care not to leave any raised edges behind), biscuit-fired and dipped in an earthenware honey glaze

- smooth grey stoneware body, covered with a layer of black slip, scratched through when it is leather-hard and fired unglazed to stoneware temperature

- a grey body covered with white slip sgraffitoed when leather-hard, bisque-fired and dipped in a transparent earthenware glaze for a very delicate finish

- grey body, biscuit-fired, covered with a rich, glossy *tenmoku* glaze, sgraffitoed while the glaze is still wet, then fired

- earthenware body, covered with black slip, biscuit-fired, dipped in shiny white majolica glaze and sgraffitoed before firing

- bisque covered with wax, sgraffitoed through to the hard pottery, and dipped in glaze of a contrasting colour and fired to the glaze temperature (the glaze will cling to the design and resist the rest)

- a bisque sample dipped in white majolica glaze, applied with a wash of underglaze colour, sgraffitoed through the colour to the glaze in some parts and to the body in others

- a bisque sample dipped in a pale stoneware glaze, applied with a thin wash of copper oxide, sgraffitoed through the oxide to the glaze and fired to stoneware

Fig. 17 *Sgraffito decoration, dancers on an Attic* oinochoe *by the Amasis Painter, c.520–515 BC. Collection Ashmolean Museum, Oxford*

- a glazed and fired sample, applied with a layer of oil-based, on-glaze colour, sgraffito through and wipe away some areas with a clean cloth. Fire again to about 750°C

Underglaze colours

In Plate 33, Sami Sanbar has very carefully tested underglaze colours by freely matching colours in concentric circles on a moulded dish. The colours were mixed with water and thinly painted over a white majolica glaze just before firing to earthenware temperature.

33 Bowl, *testing underglaze colours at earthenware temperature, by Sami Sanbar. Private collection*

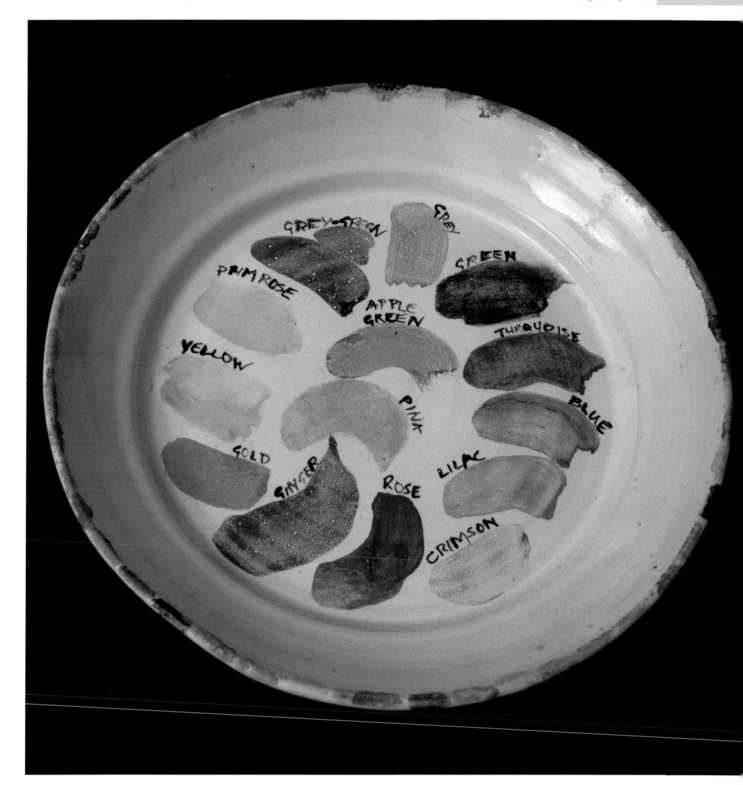

Testing the colours of slip on flat clay tiles

34 Slip colours under a clear earthenware glaze

Roll out earthenware clay on a cloth until it is evenly flat and smooth. Using a tile-cutter, template or ruler and set-square, cut out enough tiles to test each slip colour twice over. Repeat, using a smooth stoneware body.

Transfer the tiles to a smooth, dry wooden board. Take care as you do this not to bend the clay because it has what is known as a 'memory' and may bend itself back again in the kiln during the firing process. Cover the tiles with another wooden board and leave them to dry – this is the best way to ensure that they remain completely flat.

After a few hours, when the tiles are leather-hard, you can fettle the edges with a knife or damp sponge. Mark the back of each tile with a letter or number to remind yourself which colour slip you are testing, in case of surprises.

Bisque-fire and glaze with a clear earthenware glaze to bring out the full strength of the colour.

Mount the tests so that they are accessible for colour reference. You will notice that there is no optical red colour. This is because the oxides that colour the slip come from metals in order that they can withstand the heat of the kiln needed to melt the glaze.

Tests for black

	BODY	SLIP	BURNISH	BISQUE 950°c	GLAZE	Earthenware 1080°c	Stoneware 1250°c	On-glaze 750°c
1	Red	10% stain		✓				
2	Grey	10% ··		✓				
3	Red	10% ··	✓	✓				
4	Grey	10% ··	✓	✓				
5	Red	14% oxides		✓				
6	Grey	14% ··	✓	✓				
7	Red	14% ··	✓	✓				
8	Grey	14% ··	✓	✓				
9	Red	10% stain		✓	clear	✓		
10	Grey	10% ··		✓	clear		✓	
11	Red	10% ··	✓	✓	clear	✓		
12	Grey	10% ··		✓	clear		✓	
13	Red	14% oxides	✓	✓	clear	✓		
14	Grey	14% ··	✓	✓	clear		✓	
15	Red	14% ··		✓	clear	✓		
16	Grey	14% ··		✓	clear		✓	
17	Red			✓	matt black	✓		
18	Grey			✓	matt black		✓	
19	Red			✓	shiny black	✓		
20	Grey			✓	shiny black		✓	
28	Red/Grey same result			✓	unglazed – polished with 'graze' polish using soft cloth.			
29	Red			✓	clear	✓	– apply black transfer. ✓	
30	Red			✓	clear	✓	– paint on-glaze colour. ✓	
31	Red			✓	shiny black	✓	– paint egg shell lustre. ✓	
35	Black – from 10% slip		✓	✓				
36	Black – from 14% slip		✓	✓				

Fig. 18 *Tests for black, by Sandrine Glendinning*

Testing oxides on a variety of glazes

A glaze is a suspension of minerals in water. Each glaze has its own recipe and is designed to melt at a given temperature. Earthenware glazes are those which form a layer of glass on the clay surface and fire to around 1000–1100°C or cone 01. Stoneware glazes are those which combine more intimately with the clay body and mature between 1100–1300°C or cone 8.

In the oxidizing atmosphere of an electric kiln, the colour is fairly predictable but the appearance of the texture and hue will change according to the glaze and thickness of applied oxide. Oxides give clay its natural colour (see Plate 35), for instance, the red iron oxide which gives terracotta its colour on an otherwise grey body. Recipes of oxides giving slips their fired colours are given on page 87.

Once you begin to notice from your tests which oxides give strong colours and in what percentage, you can often gauge the colour of glazes by looking at the oxide content in the recipe. A note of caution about experimenting with oxide colours in earthenware glazes – the low-temperature firings may be insufficient to prevent lead release in some glazes used on vessels which contain acidic foods. The examples in Plate 35 all use stoneware glazes.

35 Oxides (rutile, tin, manganese dioxide, iron, cobalt and copper) tested on three stoneware glazes (turquoise matt, speckled white and celadon)

Kitchen materials

Non-ceramic materials are also worth testing in the heat of the kiln. The results can give a clue to their composition as well as the chance to discover materials that might provide unusual surface finishes. Plate 36 shows materials found around the house, mainly in the kitchen.

Unfired and non-ceramic finishes

There is a wide range of surface-covering materials which are suitable for non-functional ceramics but do not require firing. Wax polishes for indoor pieces are renewable. Spray paints and varnishes can give bright, long-lasting but not permanent colours. Look out for new materials with unusual colours and properties (see also page 90).

More ideas for useful tests

● how many ways can you make green, blue, yellow and white? (use the chart for black on page 63).

36 *Kitchen materials tested at earthenware temperature*

- underglaze colours
- enamels
- stoneware glazes
- a collection of different textures
- textures from a particular place
- coloured clay bodies, using body stains
- fire slip colours, unglazed to stoneware temperature
- test the full range of coloured wax polishes on white body
- alter a pale glaze by adding and testing an increasing percentage of an oxide, to a maximum of 10 per cent
- how many different ways can you apply slips?

Tests do not always have to be presented as flat shapes. The range of glaze tests by Teresa Phipps in Plate 37 uses

37 *Dinosaur glaze tests by Teresa Phipps*

miniature dinosaurs to display a range of stoneware glazes, of which some were maquettes for larger structures. These miniatures were then used as jewellery.

6
Teapots

38 Agateware, double-spouted teapot, slip-trailed King 'Lambert' and sprigged earthenware barge pot, nineteenth century. 'Valentine' teapot with slip-trailed hearts and forget-me-nots, the knob depicting a table set for two, by Mary Lambert. Artist's collection

A traditional teapot that looks good and pours well is the summit of the potter's art. A reaction to this is the movement towards making silly teapots. Perhaps it began with Robert Arneson's rude teapots which set out to shock, but today there is an abundance of anti-traditional, non-functional ware designed to amuse. It seems every animal, plant, manmade object and still-life group can be turned into a vessel to hold and dispense liquid. Try it and see how original you can be.

For inspiration, refer to the Japanese, whose tea ceremony tradition has refined the making of the implements required to a very high degree. Look also at David Leach's faceted porcelain teapots with basket handles, and Geof-frey Whiting's teapot (see Plate 39). Geoffrey Whiting was perhaps the best English teapot-maker this century and a modest man who priced his work to make it available to the ordinary household. He wanted his work to be admired in use and not set in glass cases.

The teapots illustrated here represent the best traditions of functional ware, with much of the humour of modern production.

Research

1 Simply look at and record as many different types of teapot as you can find.

2 What is the history of tea-drinking in Britain and North America?

3 What is the Japanese tea ceremony?

4 Try designing a traditional teapot, then compare the functions against the checklist opposite.

5 Draw your family's breakfast teapot in great detail.

6 Draw a cross-section of your family teapot, showing how all the parts of it relate together.

7 Collect pictures of teapots and file them according to your likes and dislikes.

8 Draw from observation as many different kinds of teapot handle as you can find.

9 Read a book about pop art.

10 Research the work of Andy Warhol.

11 Read the *Surrealism Manifesto* by André Masson.

12 Research what objects make your friends laugh.

13 Make a teapot out of another material than clay, for example, a soft sculpture sewn in cloth or terry towelling.

The traditional teapot

Make a checklist for design and function:

1 The shape of the bowl should be such that the water can have most contact with the tealeaves.

2 The base should have a raised 'foot' so that it will not scorch the table surface, and also for stability.

3 The handle should look, and be, strong enough to hold a full pot of hot liquid.

4 The handle should be big enough to hold without burning your knuckles on the hot belly.

5 The lid must fit and rest comfortably in its seating.

6 The lid flange must be long enough to wedge the lid in place when the tea is being poured.

7 The lid must have a hole in it to displace the tea and to help maintain an even flow when it is being poured out.

8 The lid should be wide enough to enable the inside of the pot to be cleaned.

9 The knob on the lid should be big enough to hold on to, without dominating the teapot design.

10 The spout should be set low enough to draw the water from just above the leaves, and long enough to extend above the lid seating so that it is not 'self-pouring', i.e. all over the tablecloth!

11 The shape of the spout should balance the profile of the handle.

12 The holes at the base of the spout should be big enough and set closely enough for the tea to flow easily through without being blocked off by tealeaves.

13 The inside must be carefully glazed so that the holes are not blocked, usually by pouring the glaze out through the spout.

39 *Classic stoneware teapot by Geoffrey Whiting. Author's collection*

40 *Modern industrial Chinese porcelain from Kwangchow. One-cup teapot with tenmoku glaze and hand-woven basket handle, by the author. Square earthenware slip-cast English teapot. Author's collection*

41 *Centring the clay*

Constructing a thrown teapot

A basic knowledge of throwing is assumed here, in that you know how to prepare the clay and centre it on the wheel. If you are not yet at this stage, try the teapots on page 71 and 72 first. You will need to set aside two sessions to make the teapot, one for the throwing and another for assembling the leather-hard forms.

42 *Making the seating for the lid*

Throwing the body and seating

Prepare a ball of smooth plastic clay by wedging or kneading. Centre the clay in a square cross-section with a flat top and straight sides. Make a hole in the middle with your thumb, leaving a generous 1 cm thickness of clay for the base. Open out the form to make a thick cylinder, taking care to keep the clay wall an even thickness.

Carefully push out the belly of the pot so that the clay thins to its final form and thickness; the rim should be still narrower and double the thickness of the rest of the clay wall. Using a rib, divide the rim into two, making a right angle (see Plate 42) which will form the seating for the lid. Measure each part of this seating with callipers. Use the measurements to adjust the thrown lids so that they are as close-fitting as possible.

43 *Throwing the lid upside down*

Throwing the lid

This must be thrown at the same time as the pot base if the measurements are to be accurate. A teapot lid is traditionally thrown upside down, in the form of a small bowl with a divided rim and thick base from which to turn the knob. Divide the rim with a right-angled rib in the same way as the teapot base. Measure these extensions carefully with callipers to ensure that they will fit the seating snugly in every direction. The lid should extend into the teapot for about 2 cm (¾ in) so that it will wedge itself in place and not fall out when the last cup is being poured.

44 *Collaring the spout*

Collaring the spout

Throw several, unless you already know by experience how tall the spout needs to be. A big mistake is to throw short spouts which pour out water while the water is still pouring in. Throw a narrow cylinder, then collar it (see Plate 44) until it is less than finger-wide.

45 *Turning the base*

Turning the teapot base

When all the parts are leather-hard, begin to assemble them. Turn the base by fixing it upside down on a wheel-head with a roll of clay. Start by trimming off any unevenness. The base should be slightly concave, so that the teapot will nest on the 'foot' left by the raised outer edge.

46 *Turning the knob*

Turning the knob

Fix the leather-hard lid the correct way up on the wheel-head with rolls of clay. Carefully turn the knob on the top from the extra thick base, left after throwing. When it is a shape that is comfortable to hold, test it by taking it off the wheel and lifting it in and out of the teapot seating. If the fit is generally too tight, carefully trim the lid by turning but make a mental note to measure more carefully next time.

Remember to make a small hole in the lid for the air to displace the tea and make for smooth pouring.

47 *Fitting the cut and trimmed spout in place over the strainer holes*

Fitting the spout

Look at the teapot and its lid in profile. Hold the spout in the position you want it, making sure that when the top of the spout is cut straight you can fill the teapot without it overflowing.

Cut the base of the spout parallel with the teapot belly and neaten it on the inside if it is thicker than the rest. Mark on the teapot belly where it is to be fixed and cut out a pattern of holes between the marks, to make a strainer. Fix the spout in place with some slurry and check from every angle that it is placed centrally. Model the spout carefully into the teapot form and finish by sponging over the joined surfaces.

48 *Fitting the pulled handle*

Fitting the handle

Attach the handle before it stiffens, using thick slurry to join it to the teapot. Press both ends firmly in place. Check from above and below that the handle is centred and model it in place so that it seems to grow out of the pot.

The most important things about a teapot handle are that it is fixed on firmly enough to hold a full pot of tea, that it *looks* strong enough and that the space between the handle and the body is pleasing.

Fig. 20 is a cross-section of how your teapot should fit together as a balanced whole. The inset shows the pattern of holes made in the pot wall to let the tea into the spout. When you are designing traditional teapots, it is helpful to draw the section through in this way and check that a vital aspect has not been overlooked. It is also an excellent professional discipline to imagine your work from the inside, and how its form relates to the function.

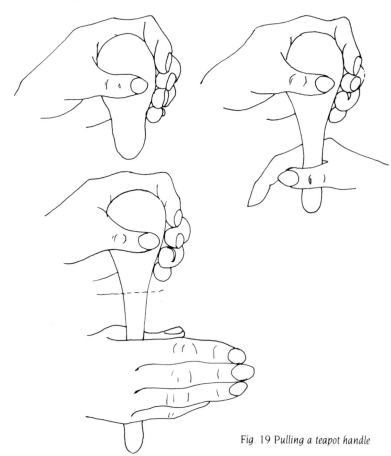

Fig. 19 *Pulling a teapot handle*

Pulling the handle

Take a piece of soft clay the size and shape of a pear, wet the thinner end and slowly stroke it downwards between your thumb and the base of your first finger. As the clay elongates, keep it as even as possible by alternating the strokes with your thumb, first on one side and then the other. When the handle is as thin as the rest of the teapot and wide enough to look strong, pinch it off and leave it to set while you make alternatives.

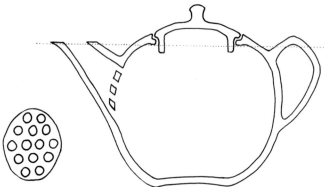

Fig. 20 *Teapot cross-section. (Inset) Sieve pattern*

Fig. 21 *Designs for humorous teapots, by Jameson Davis*

49 English seaside giftware teapot in the form of a shell. Author's collection

It takes time to learn to throw a perfect centred pot. In the meantime, you may want to try a different style of working. Wedge the clay and start to centre it. While it is still off-centre, however, make the hole in the centre with your thumb and take it from there, aiming for spontaneity and asymmetry.

Humorous teapots

Plates 49 and 50 are examples of designs you may uncover. They show the lively, humorous influence of pop art and Surrealism, art movements which set out to make us see symbolic meanings in everyday objects – soup cans, loaves of bread, images of Marilyn Monroe or an umbrella.

For a really silly teapot, many or all of the points on page 67 could be disregarded. They might even serve as a list of what *not* to do. Perhaps there are well-known museum pieces behind glass because someone forgot to put holes at the base of the spout!

Other teapot designs

1   Design some very silly, non-functional teapots.

2   Design a teapot that looks like a letter of the alphabet.

3   Design a milk jug, sugar bowl and cup to go with your teapot.

4   Design a teapot that looks like a dinosaur.

5   Re-design an everyday manmade object as a humorous teapot.

6   Design a teapot with absolutely none of the correct functions in the checklist on page 67.

7   Consider what object makes you laugh the most and make a teapot depicting that.

8   Ask a ten-year-old schoolchild to design a teapot based on what makes him or her laugh.

9   Make a paper sculpture of a teapot and use it as templates to construct a slab pot.

10   Draw your family as a set of teapots.

If you know how to make a teapot lid, you could also make a ginger jar, a casserole or a carved stopper. Another way to make a lid is to throw an enclosed form and cut away an angled lid when it is leather-hard.
If you can pull a handle, you can also make mugs, cups, basket-handle supports and lugs (fix them on sideways). Other ways to make handles are coiling (single, double or plaited), cutting a thin strip from a clay slab, extruding (pushing them through a wad box die plate) and cutting a hole from the rim of the pot.

50 Mass-produced Chinese porcelain 'cat and fish' teapot with on-glaze painted decoration. Collection Rosalind Bliss

51 Jug by Gilles Le Corre, with brushed and trailed glazes

7.
Holiday projects

One of the marvellous aspects of pottery is that no matter where in the world you travel there are potters. Each country has made its contribution to the craft and looking round museums the skill and versatility of potters throughout the ancient world are an inspiration. The inheritance of their work is still available to us, thanks to the durability of the clay material which, given good conditions, can look as fresh today as when it was first produced many hundreds of years ago, for example Chinese porcelain of the Tang dynasty (618–907 AD).

You may have chosen a ceramic culture to study and have already thoroughly researched it in libraries and museums. Alternatively, your holiday may have arisen for social reasons and you want to take the opportunity to explore the ceramic activity in a particular region. Using the inquisitiveness of a good detective, the international language of pots is there for you to discover. It helps to be prepared before your holiday:

1 Study the locality. Where are the pots likely to be? What other ceramic articles would you expect to see? Plan a visit to a nearby pottery. What is its history and origins? From where does it draw its inspiration? How long is its history?

2 Contact the nearest pottery manufacturers of tiles or sanitary fitments. Do they have open days? Would they show you around? What machinery is used during the processes? Do they keep a small museum of past products?

3 Check your drawing and photographic equipment. It should not be too bulky but take what you like to use.

4 Talk or write to other potters who have been to the same area and note what they found unusual or unexpected.

5 Pick a future holiday spot and study the pottery there. Appreciate the joys of armchair travelling!

52 *The Temple of Heaven, Peking*

China

China has perhaps the longest ceramic history in terms of what is still available to us today. The expertise of the Ancient Chinese kiln-builders produced the first glazed white pottery. This ware was in great demand and was transported along trade routes by camel and donkey. The new technology spread throughout the Persian Empire, finding its way to Spain with the invading Moors. This is the root of Hispano-Moresque lustreware, Italian majolica, French faïence, Dutch delftware and English whiteware.

The pagodas illustrated on page 78 belong to the Han dynasty (206 BC–AD 220), when glaze technology in China was still in its infancy. They are currently housed in the Historical Museum in Peking but there are many other similar, well-documented examples in museums around the world.

Today the evidence of a rich ceramic history is every-

53 Tile panel from the Forbidden City, Peking

54 Entrance to the Shrine of the Sleeping Buddha, near Peking

where in China. It is part of the architecture, in the form of colourful roof tiles on older buildings, pagodas, temples, memorials, etc. Potters produce domestic ware in small factories and 'art pottery' in the manner of the best (and worst) traditions of the past. Cooking pots, night soil containers, portable charcoal stoves, decorative wall panels, dragon sculptures and lidded tea mugs are all part of modern China and a growing export trade.

Research

1 When you arrive in China, note or draw all the unusual ceramic objects and study their *forms*.

2 What colours are used, what oxides, slides and clays?

3 Try to work out how objects are made. Are there obvious throwing rings or side seams, which would indicate moulding, a popular Chinese method?

4 What sort of pattern work do you find on the ceramic work? Is it part of the form, incised, modelled or inlaid, or is it applied with slip, oxides or glazes?

5 Amongst the wealth of material you will find, make a collection in pictures or drawings of one item, e.g. coloured wall panels or plant pots.

6 Ask a guide if there are any kilns locally.

7 Collect pictures of Chinese dragons in as many media as possible – stone, wood, clay, embroidery, etc.

8 Learn the dynasties by heart and teach yourself to recognize the ceramic styles associated with each one.

9 Plan a series of your own work, showing a Chinese influence. This might mean the use of a certain glaze or decorative style.

The Model Army

Probably the greatest archaeological find in China was the discovery in 1974 of the ancient tomb of Ch'in Shih Huang-ti, containing a model army. The soldiers, horses and war machines are life size, hollow and made in moulded sections of fired and painted clay.

The soldiers' expressions are stern. Moulds from different expressions could be interchanged, with other complete heads fitting into different necks. The bodies were built from the ground upwards – feet to knees, knees to waist and waist to neck. Different hand moulds, to hold real weapons, make up each soldier from a kit of interchangeable moulds.

The whole army, containing hundreds of figures, is dated 221–206BC in the Chin dynasty, which immediately predates the Han.

1 Using this method of large-scale construction, design and make a large-scale figure for yourself. You could depict someone from history or a person in modern dress. Viola Frey in America makes life-sized modern figures which express a powerful social comment.

2 Throw a series of small bowls on a wheel. When they are leather-hard, arrange them one on top of the other like a circular temple. Fix them together like slab pots by scoring and slipping. Turn over the completed single form and cut out doors, windows, pattern work, etc.

3 Make a square slabbed dish with square slabbed feet to house a collection of small indoor plants, like cactus or bonsai.

4 Make ten small maquettes of Chinese dragon-dogs. Coil-build one of them on a larger scale and glaze it with an oxide coloured earthenware glaze.

5 Make a panel of low-relief tiles based on a dragon or a lotus flower, or the patterns made by paddy fields.

Pagodas

The pagodas on page 78 were slab-built from a textured body. Each floor was constructed separately and the floors were then stacked on top of each other, but not joined. They were probably assembled like this inside the kiln, and did not fuse together because they were unglazed.

To make a pagoda, it is best to construct it first out of paper which can later be carefully deconstructed to use as the template.

Roll out the clay and let it stiffen between two boards. Cut out the walls, with holes for windows, doors and decorative pattern work. Carefully assemble the cut and

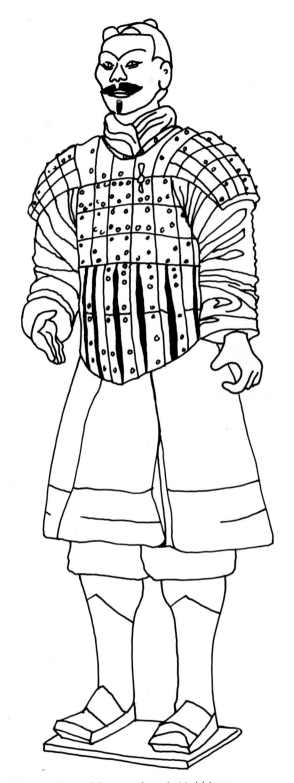

Fig. 22 Foot soldier in full armour from the Model Army

Fig. 23 Han pagodas from the Historical Museum in Peking

pierced slabs, mitring the corners as shown on page 24.

When the leather-hard structure is assembled, add details of modelled figures and objects. Decorate with impressed patterns and/or painted slip. Dry the whole structure as slowly and evenly as possible to prevent cracking, then biscuit-fire to a higher temperature, making the clay harder and more permanent.

A pagoda looks particularly good in a natural outdoor setting when the surface has acquired the patina of a season's weathering.

Celtic knotwork

A holiday in Scotland, Ireland or northern France would give you the opportunity to study this rich source of pattern work. Similar forms of interlaced patterns based on mathematical construction can be seen in the Ukraine and Yugoslavia, dated thousands of years BC.

Interwoven patterns reach their highest form in the manuscripts of the Book of Kells and the Lindisfarne Gospels. They are also to be found in all forms of craftwork and architectural detail where the Celts lived.

1   Make a frieze of tiles with a Celtic knotwork pattern incised in low relief.

2   Make a plain slab-built box and carve a Celtic motif into the lid.

3   Unravel one knot and make it the basis of a slip-trailed design on a large bowl.

4   Translate a tiny part of an interwoven pattern into a three-dimensional construction. Make a series of small maquettes before interpreting one of them in a large-scale coiled structure.

5   Compose a wise saying about the labyrinth of a knot and write it, graffiti-style, over a very simple form.

6   Bisque-fire a small section of low-relief knotwork. Use this stamp to impress on other work.

7   Construct a knotwork pattern from coils. Roll over it lightly with a rolling pin until it joins together well enough to make a slab. Finish drying it in a shaped plaster mould.

8   Use the method above to produce a kinetic sculpture.

9   Paint a knotwork border on a majolica plate.

10   Carve a tiny porcelain brooch showing a knotwork creature.

Fig. 24 *Village monument, Lochgilphead, Scotland*

79

Fig. 25 Celtic knotwork

Italy

Italy has a rich ceramic tradition of painted white pottery which dates back to the fourteenth century. Spanish potters, influenced by the Moorish invasion of their country, brought to Italy their ideas for a pure white pottery, like Chinese porcelain, covered with rich painted pattern work and imagery. The trade route came from China through Persia into Spain and thence to Renaissance Italy, where the technology and designs involved were written down and clearly drawn by Cipriano Piccolpasso in his *Three Books of the Potter's Art*.

Throughout Italy today you can see the most beautiful painted white pottery, or *maiolica*, in the churches, houses, as public wall plaques and still manufactured for sale in centres such as Deruta. The colourful plate shown on page 82 is a typical example from the fifteenth century where the painted surface has taken over in importance from the form. There was a particular fashion in Florence for portrait dishes of important people, set within a patterned frame based on foliage or peacock feathers.

Fig. 26 shows an *albarello*, or medicine jar, found on the shelves of an apothecary's shop.

Fig. 26 *Design for an* albarello

55 Majolica portrait dish from Gubbio. Collection Ashmolean Museum,
Oxford

Majolica

This is the standard English form of *maiolica* and describes what we know as tin-glazed earthenware. The body is a soft, low-fired buff colour, the glaze as shiny and opaque as possible through the addition of tin oxide to a lead base. The recipe on page 87 gives a safer version, using lead bisilicate as a frit.

The decoration is painted blue, from cobalt oxide, or a variety of other colours: green from copper, yellows from iron oxide and plummy browns from manganese. You might experiment with some Chinese long-haired brushes to see the possible range of marks on a dry, powdery surface. The biscuit-fired ware is dipped in white glaze before the oxide painting. Rehearse your design carefully before starting, using watercolours on fine blotting paper to get an idea of how fast you will need to work. Aim for relaxed speed, so that the brush takes up the flow of the design and apparent imperfections are acceptable within that rhythm.

Other Italian sources of inspiration

As well as the rich historical tradition of ceramics, sculpture and architecture, look at the landscapes of Italy which are shaped by the history and traditions of society as much as the towns and cities. How could you use the thumbnail sketches of Italian vineyards in Fig. 27? As painted borders for a majolica plate? Or as a starting point for brushwork motifs?

Twentieth-century design still sets the fashion in Italy and the work of Ettore Sottsass and his Memphis School are very influential. The Memphis ceramic designer is Matteo Thun, whose brightly coloured post-Modernism is worth searching out.

Faenza is an important ceramic town. It has a major pottery collection and hosts an international ceramic competition. From Naples to Venice you will find beautiful majolica ware and potters at work using the latest technology as well as traditional techniques.

56 Modern tin-glazed earthenware dish, with cobalt oxide painted decoration, by Suzanne Lang. Private collection

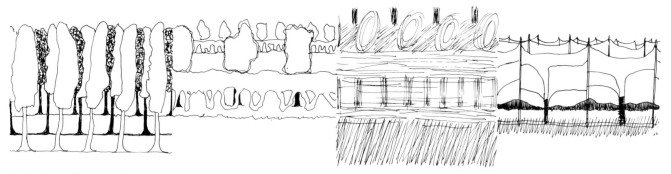

Fig. 27 Designs from an Italian vineyard

More ideas

1   From an illustration, make as exact a replica as you can of a Florentine majolica portrait dish.

2   Make a painted majolica Christmas crib, with modelled figures of Mary, Joseph, the animals, etc.

3   Make a majolica portrait dish of a friend, a child or a pop star.

4   Make a set of bathroom or kitchen splashback tiles in painted majolica.

5   Using Chinese brushes, letter a simple poem on a large moulded dish. Use cobalt oxide on top of tin glaze.

6   Make a test tile of as wide a colour range of oxides on majolica glaze as you have available.

7   Draw all the ceramic objects you see where you are staying. Research how they are made. Include washbasins, doorknobs, etc. Could you make any of these?

8   Make a set of contemporary *albarelli* to contain a specific set of materials.

9   Make a set of tiles with polychrome oxide decorative painting.

10   Paint a blue vineyard on a single white tile.

Key words in other languages

English	clay	glaze	kiln	pottery	earthenware	stoneware	porcelain	slip	oxides	enamels	the potter	potter's wheel
French	l'argille	l'émail	le four	la poterie	terre cuite	le grès	la porcelaine	la barotine	les oxides	l'émaux	le potier	le tour
Italian	la terra	vetri	il forno	la ceramica	terracotta	il crete	la porcelana	l'engobe	ossido	lo smalto	vasaio	ruota del vasaio
Spanish	pastas	cubiertas	el horno	la ceramica	loza	gres	la porcelana	barbotina	oxido	esmaltado	—	el torno
Chinese (pinyin)	tao tu	shang you	yoo	—	tao qi	shi qi	ci qi	hua ni	yang hua wu	ci you	zhi tao gong ren	—
Japanese	nendo	yuyaku	gama	yakimono	doki	sekki	jiki	deisho	sanka	uwae	togeika, toko	rokuro

Glossary

APPLIED DECORATION clay added on to the form for decorative purposes

BATT a shelf of kiln furniture, composed of a reinforced high-firing body

BISCUIT/BISQUE the English name for 'bisque', the first low-temperature firing of a pot in the kiln, between 750–1000°C, cones 16–5

CLAY BODY the clay material

CHAMBER internal kiln dimensions

CHUCK a turning support (see page 88)

CONES small pyramids of ceramic material, formulated to bend when a certain point is reached in the firing cycle

EARTHENWARE a type of low-fired pottery, often with a shiny, coloured glaze skin

FETTLE to trim or smooth over a join in the surface of a moulded pot

FIRECLAY a coarse clay used for bricks and making grog

FLUX any material that lowers the melting point of a glaze, e.g. an oxide

FOOT a raised edge at the base of a pot, on which it stands

FRIT glaze materials pre-fired and ground to make them safe, e.g. lead and silica into lead bisilicate

GLAZE initially, a suspension of chemicals that will become glass when subjected to the heat of the kiln

GROG a pre-fired and ground material made from fireclay

INCISED DECORATION low-relief carving into the leather-hard clay surface

INLAY a technique of decoration where incised patterns are filled in with a contrasting colour of clay, glaze or oxide

KIDNEY a rubber or metal smoothing tool shaped like a kidney

KILN a potter's furnace

LAWN the mesh of a sieve, fastened to the frame

LEATHER-HARD the state of the clay where it is stiff but not yet dry

LIP the top rim of a vessel

LUSTRES transparent on-glaze colours composed of metallic salts in a binding material

MAJOLICA shiny white earthenware glaze containing tin oxide

MAQUETTE small three-dimensional study for a larger piece of sculptural work

NERIAGE laminated clay built into slabs, usually in a mould

ON-GLAZE COLOURS China paint or enamels, oil-based oxide colours painted on the glaze-fired ware then re-fired

OXIDES heat-resistant colouring materials derived from metals

PLASTIC CLAY the clay body, soft but not sticky

RAKU a method of low-temperature fast firing

REDUCTION the kiln atmosphere is 'reduced', or deprived of oxygen, by the introduction of fuel into the closed firing chamber

SGRAFFITO a method of decoration involving scratching through one layer of colour to reveal another

SLAKE soaking dry clay lumps in water to soften them

SLIP liquid clay, often with oxide colour added for decoration

SLURRY mushy unsieved slip used to join clay slabs

STONEWARE a type of higher fired pottery

TEMPLATE a cut-out shape of cardboard or wood used as a pattern for cutting out slabs of clay

TERRA SIGILLATA a very fine slip (see page 59)

TERRACOTTA literally 'cooked earth', brown earthenware pottery

THROWING the activity of making a pot on the potter's wheel

THROWING RIB shaped wooden form used in throwing

THUMB POTS small bowls made by pinching the clay between thumb and finger (see page 14)

TRANSFERS designs pre-printed on glaze oxide colours

TURNING trimming a leather-hard pot while spinning it on the potter's wheel

UNDERGLAZE COLOURS transparent oxide colours applied on top of the glaze before the glaze firing

57 'The Sailors' Farewell', lustreware jug, Sunderland, late eighteenth century. Transfer-decorated. Collection Mary Lambert

Technical notes

Recipes

All clay bodies, slips, colours and glazes have a recipe, known or unknown. The composition of some naturally occurring materials is still the subject of scientific and archaeological formulae; equally successful results can be achieved with the empirical cup-and-spoon method as our foremothers did in the kitchen, that original chemist's shop. Industry has a tradition of keeping recipes secret, and ceramic industrialists like Josiah Wedgwood used to go to extraordinary lengths to guard the secrets of their most beautiful wares.

Where will your recipes come from? You could start from scratch, following the examples in chapter 5, or you could refer to the specialist books available (see pages 90–91). Manufacturers' catalogues often give recipes, or you could talk to other potters in your locality who might help you to interpret interesting, locally available materials.

You could take these recipes and gradually adapt them to your requirements and taste. Remember that recipes do not automatically transpose from one place to another, mainly because mined materials are likely to differ slightly. The following recipes are offered on the understanding that you test them before using, and look carefully at the suitability of the accompanying body or glaze. All the recipes are expressed in parts (100 gm makes a jamjar-sized test of 250 gm, while 2 kg makes a small bucketful).

Health and safety

Although no directly poisonous materials are used here, it is wise to observe some general precautions. Dust is the main hazard – fine particles are not visible but could still affect your lungs.

1 Keep dry materials in lidded containers – not dusty packets. Label them carefully.

2 Always add materials *to* water, not the other way round.

3 Wear an apron so that dust does not impregnate your clothes. Remember to wash it regularly.

4 Keep any open wounds covered up while you handle the materials, or wear rubber gloves.

Body recipes

Egyptian paste (turquoise, self-glazing, Cone 08–4 temp.)

bicarbonate of soda	20
flint	40

bentonite 40
copper carbonate 5

Dry-sift through an 80-mesh sieve. (Remember to wear a mask.) Add water just before use.

A typical clay body (white earthenware)

ball clay 5
China clay 5
flint 6
feldspar 4

Soak in water overnight. If there are lumps, sieve through a 40-mesh sieve; otherwise, mix thoroughly, drain and wedge. If you keep it for a while before using it, the plasticity will increase – a week makes a difference, a month is even better.

Porcelain

China clay 55
feldspar 25
quartz 15
bentonite 5

St Thomas body (stoneware)

red body 60
fireclay 30

A raku body

red body 30
fireclay 40
fire grog 40

Slip recipes

White slip

ball clay 100
or
white earthenware 100
Slake then sieve through 80-mesh lawn.
or
flint 6
ball clay 5
China clay 5
feldspar 4

Other colours

ball clay 50
China clay 50
body stain 5–10
(available in a variety of colours – see your manufacturer's catalogue)

Yellow slip

ball clay 50

yellow ochre 3
lemon yellow stain 3

Black slip

ball clay 100
black iron oxide 7
manganese 5
cobalt 2

Green slip

ball clay 100
copper oxide 5

Blue slip

ball clay 100
cobalt oxide 2
copper oxide 1

Red slip

ball clay 50
red clay 25
red iron oxide 25
or
terracotta body

Glaze recipes

Earthenware clear glaze (transparent) Cone 01, 1080°C

lead bisilicate 74
ball clay 13
flint 9
whiting 4
bentonite 2

Earthenware majolica (shiny white) Cone 01, 1080°C

lead bisilicate 38.4
borax frit 19.7
tin oxide 4
zinc oxide 8
China clay 14

Earthenware honey glaze (transparent yellow) Cone 01, 1080°C

lead bisilicate 100
red clay 35

Wood ash glaze (often greeny, speckled and semi-matt) Cone 8, 1250°C

Wood ash glaze is a good one to make after a bonfire or to use wood ash saved from a fire grate. Keep a note of the type of wood burnt as each gives a different glaze – fruit woods are particularly favoured. Soak the wood ash in an enamel bucket and remove anything that floats or falls heavily to the bottom – use rubber gloves as the mixture is quite alkaline. Sieve the ash through 60-, then 100-mesh lawn. Wash it, filling the bucket with water and letting the ash settle, then pour it off from the top; repeat until the water is clear.

Stoneware tenmoku (Shiny black, breaking brown) Cone 8, 1250°C

Cornish stone 88
whiting 12
iron oxide 8

Stoneware celadon (jade green, semi-transparent) Cone 8, 1250°C

feldspar 40
flint 30
whiting 20
China clay 10
iron oxide 4

Stoneware pebble (matt white/grey) Cone 8, 1250°C

China clay 25
potash feldspar 50
white 5

Economy mixture (test and see) Cone 8, 1250°C

Mix together any scraps of unfired glaze samples or remains of glaze buckets in the studio. Sieve the mixture and if it settles firmly add a spoonful of bentonite. Test by firing – if it runs add a handful of ball clay, adding more until the test shows a stiffer result.

Throwing

How do I learn to throw a pot?

You will need access to a potter's wheel, some plastic clay and a potter to demonstrate. You cannot learn throwing from a book, but reading about it can help your understanding of the processes involved and pictures are good examples (see chapter 6).

Why is it called throwing?

Probably because the force of the spinning wheel tries to throw the clay off, as water will

58 *Throwing a cylinder*

demonstrate. Your hands shape the pot by counteracting this force.

What is the best sort of clay for throwing?

A fine-grained plastic body. I would recommend a terracotta earthenware for economy and versatility. A St Thomas body will give you confidence with larger forms.

How do I begin?

Assemble the tools and materials you will need on the potter's wheel: bowl of water, cheese wire, natural sponge, spike for trimming, wooden board, wooden ribs and several balls of wedged clay.

How do I know when the clay is centred?

Press your hands slowly and firmly over the form to flatten the top and straighten the sides. The clay should now appear to be still while it is still spinning. If it does not, wet it again and keep pressing.

How do I make it into a bowl or cylinder?

Slowly make a well in the centre of the form with one or both thumbs. Pull the clay wall between your thumb and finger outwards to make a bowl, and upwards to make a cylinder. Your hands must stay in the same position for at least one complete wheel revolution for the pot to remain even.

Can I even up an uneven top?

Yes. Use the spike to gradually pierce the clay wall and, supported by two fingers inside the pot, take off at least a centimetre all round. Flip off the cut circle and even up the new lip with a slight finger-pressure down.

How do I get the form off the wheel?

By sliding it on a pool of water after you have cut it through at the base with a stretched wire, *or* by lifting with four fingers at the base after you have cut it through.

What do I do to it next?

Leave it to go leather-hard. This might take overnight in a damp cupboard, or a couple of hours on a warm summer's day. To be ready for turning, it should be stiff but not dry.

How do I get it off the board?

If it has stuck because it is not leather-hard yet, leave it longer. If it is leather-hard, pick up the pot by the base and tap the board vertically on the table, taking care not to distort the pot. Cut the base with a taut wire, but be prepared to lose some clay from the bottom of the pot.

What is a chuck?

A thrown, or turned, leather-hard cylinder of clay used to support the shoulders of a bottle during turning.

How do I know when the pot is turned to an even thickness?

By estimating with your thumb and finger, by measuring with callipers, by cutting a test piece in half with a wire to check your ability to estimate thickness, by feeling where the weight is when you pick it up, or by judging visually, inside and out.

Can I decorate it now?

Yes (see page 89).

When can I fire it?

As soon as it is bone dry.

What shall I do next?

Practise throwing cylinders. These are like scales for a singer. A good thrower can do one of at least 25 cm (10 in). Take every chance you can to watch experienced throwers, it will train your eye in good practice.

Decorating

A variety of methods of decoration have been mentioned in this book, either in the projects or in suggestions for designs. The choice of design is up to you, and you will need to work out when it is technically possible to use the decorative method you have chosen and to time carefully when the clay (and you) are in the correct state. Table 1 describes the uses of traditional decorating materials and the following pages give suggestions for other possibilities.

Glazing bisque

Keep the work dust-free. Try to handle it as little as possible, otherwise greasy finger marks will

When to decorate TABLE I (Read from the bottom upwards)

Body state	Decoration		Next Process
Glaze-fired	Paint with acrylics, spray with oil-based paints, gold, etc.		
	On-glaze colours, painted, sprayed, sgraffito, etc. Lustres, painted, sprayed Transfer colours and decals		Re-fire to 750°C
	Oxide wash over a crackle glaze		Re-fire earthware or stoneware
Glaze-dipped bisque	Stencilled oxide or underglaze colours Sgraffito through glaze to the body Sgraffito through oxide to the glaze Painted, sprayed or splashed oxide colours Painted, sprayed or splashed underglaze colours Painted, sprayed or splashed with other glazes		Fire earthware or stoneware
Bisque-fired	Wax-resist decoration Underglaze colours, if glaze spraying Thinly painted slip		Apply glaze and fire
	Oxide wash or inlay into incised decoration, thinly painted slip (*hakeme*), glaze painting, dipping, spraying, splashing, inlay, etc.		Fire earthware or stoneware
	Coloured, plain or scented surface wax or oil		Re-fire in sawdust kiln or bonfire, for black flashes
Dry	Wire wool or metal kidney over neriage NB The body is extremely fragile		Fire to bisque
Leather-hard	Burnishing Incising Cut work Sprigging Turning Scraping (to raise grog for a textured surface)	With slip: Trailing Tube lining Sgraffito Inlay Paint Stencils Spongeing	Dry evenly then fire to bisque
Plastic clay body	Slip-dipping, trailing, feathering and stencilling (if supported) Slip-painting and combing Applied clay and sprigging (if supported) Impressed patterns (organic, inorganic) Impressed textures or bisque stamps Decorative coiling Neriage Modelled surfaces		Dry evenly

prevent the glaze from adhering.
The style of decoration, the size of the pot and the amount of glaze available will determine the method of use. Stir the glaze right from the bottom and sieve out any lumps. Mop up any spilt glaze before it dries to prevent inhaling potentially dangerous dust.

and coloured glazes show finger marks, so hold the pot where they will not show or wipe that area clean with a damp sponge. If you cannot do the inside and outside together, you could pour the inside first and then dip the outside. Alternatively, paint liquid wax on the bottom of the pot to prevent it being glazed.

Glaze the inside first by filling it up with glaze and quickly pouring it out. For the outside, use a container wider than the base of the bisque to catch the drips. Place two sticks or rolling guides over the container and put the pot on top. Take a jug of freshly stirred glaze and pour it evenly round the form in a single layer.

Dipping

This is the quickest and easiest method if you have a big tub of glaze and a small pot. Opaque

Pouring

This is a good method if the pot is large, the amount of glaze limited or you want a different glaze on the outside.

Spraying

This is the only method to use if unfired oxides or underglaze colours have been painted directly onto the bisque.

Unless you intend to work outside, you will need spraying equipment with a spray booth, extractor, etc. Spraying is a potentially dangerous practice because fine particles are released into the air, so wear a protective mask. The glaze may have to be thinned for spraying; make sure you build up a thick enough layer by putting the pot on a banding wheel and gradually rotating it as you spray. This method is also useful for achieving subtle colour changes, adding a thin layer of colour oxides or another glaze.

Painting

This is a good way to apply glazes to bisque for decorative purposes. Although it will not produce an even layer, brushmarks add texture and movement to a design (see Gilles Le Corre's pot on page 74).

An all-over painted pattern on a plain form could have the richness of a Janice Tchalenko pot. A painted or sponged glaze decoration on a dipped, sprayed or poured base might glow with colour, like those she designed for her Dart Pottery tableware. Painted colours can also complete a tube-lined surface by flooding in the glazes between the divisions of the pattern.

Kilns

Kilns can be categorized by their shape, the type of fuel used to fire them, the direction the draft of heated air takes inside the kiln and the type of ware being fired.

Shapes

Bank kiln a single-chamber kiln scooped out of a low earth bank, with the fire mouth at the bottom and the chimney opening at the top (early Chinese)

Bonfire kiln a mound of pots on the ground with fuel (often dried animal dung) heaped around them, then set alight (African)

Bottle kiln a room-sized, brick-built chamber with a chimney giving it the characteristic bottle form (nineteenth century, Staffordshire)

Catenary arch a modern arch-shaped kiln making optimum use of a downdraft firing pattern (American)

Dragon arch an anagama or climbing kiln, consisting of several linked chambers built on a slope. At night the fire and smoke from the many stokeholes make it look like a dragon (Korean/Japanese/Chinese)

Pedestal kiln the chamber floor is supported by a pedestal, with the fire underneath and the draft rising upwards through the ware (early Roman)

Tunnel kiln the ware is placed on a moving trolley which slowly progresses through the tunnel, heated continuously to firing temperature in the middle (Western industrial)

Fuel

Coal household coal, or charcoal for smaller kilns

Electric used for industrial to portable studio-sized kilns

Gas using town or bottled gas

Oil-fired drip-fed, often using oil waste

Salt a salt kiln is a solid fuel kiln with a reduced temperature produced by the addition of salt which volatilizes to form a glaze on the raw ware (and the inside of the kiln), releasing chrome gas into the atmosphere

Sawdust a sawdust kiln is a small brick-built container filled with sawdust and pots (see Fig. 28), which is lit from the top, covered and left for several hours to produce attractive black bisque ware

Split bamboo used to reduce the atmosphere when fed into the spyhole of a sealed, solid-fuel-fired kiln

Wood the most commonly used fuel in the past but fast becoming ecologically unsound

Updraft where the warm air from the fire mouth at the base of the kiln rises through the ware to the top, as in pedestal, bank and bottle kilns

Downdraft where the warm air rises, but in order to escape through the chimney entrance is drawn downwards again while the heat is built up, as in most gas-fired, dragon and climbing kilns

Ware

Brick kilns structures purely for firing, where the fuels are introduced between quite tightly packed bricks

Raku small chambered kilns, often portable, for fast firing in less than an hour. The ware is lifted out red hot with tongs and cooled in water or sawdust (originally Japanese)

Test kilns for firing glaze and body samples in a few hours in a chamber about 30 cm (1 ft) square

Packing a biscuit kiln

When you pack a biscuit kiln, you are aiming to fill the inside of the kiln as evenly as possible without leaving any empty spaces, like a three-dimensional jigsaw puzzle.

The electrical elements will build up a protective, powdery layer which must not be disturbed while you are working in the kiln. Place the ware to allow for heat expansion *at least 2.5 cm (1 in)*

Finishing Ceramic Sculpture

Medium	Advantages	Disadvantages
Shiny glazes	Easy to clean; indoor or outdoor use	Light reflections show up unevennesses of the form
Matt glazes	Earthenware or stoneware; indoor or outdoor use	Brighter colours may detract from the form; the glaze fills in and flattens the modelling
Vitrified clay	Good natural colours, modelling shows clearly; indoor or outdoor use	None
Wax polishes	A variety of colours available	Will need repolishing from time to time; only indoor use
Metal polish	Available in bronze, gold and silver finishes	Cost may be a factor; only indoor use
Paints (acrylic/spray/house)	Good colour range	The ceramic surface texture is covered over
Oxide wash	Highlights details of the form; indoor and outdoor use	None
Natural patina (e.g. moss)	Blends with the outdoor environment	Patina may change seasonally

from the elements. You can put three or four pieces inside or on top of one another, but wider plates need sand between them to allow for the movement of shrinkage and expansion.

Align the kiln furniture stilts on top of each other, through the layers of batts, to prevent them warping in the heat. Fill up the kiln layer by layer, being very careful how you handle the brittle, dry pots. Do not put any (even slightly) damp pots in the kiln, because the steam they would produce is damaging.

Packing a glaze kiln

The difference with a glaze kiln is that the pots must be separated from each other because, just as the glaze fuses to the clay body, it could do the same to another pot or the kiln shelf. *Kissing* is where two pots touch and fuse; *setting* is the careful placing of pots so that this does not happen. It is also advisable to check that enough glaze has been cleaned from the bases.

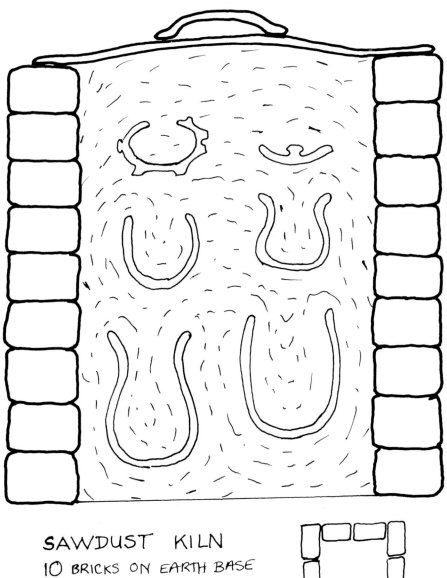

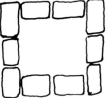

SAWDUST KILN
10 BRICKS ON EARTH BASE
9 LAYERS HIGH
= 90 BRICKS.

Fig. 28

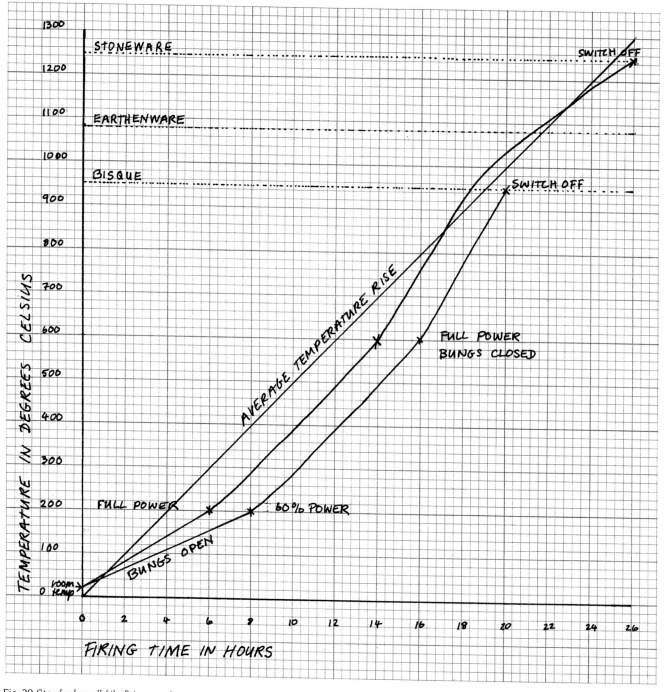

Fig. 29 Standard small kiln firing graph

Further reading

Handbuilding

Berensohn, Paulus, *Finding one's way with clay. Pinched pottery and the colour of clay*, Simon and Schuster, 1972

Blandino, Betty, *Coiled Pottery: traditional and contemporary ways*, A. & C. Black, 1984

Speight, Charlotte F., *Images in Clay Sculpture: historical and contemporary techniques*, Harper & Row, 1983

Waller, Jane, *Handbuilt Ceramics*, B. T. Batsford, 1990

Throwing

Casson, Michael, *The Craft of the Potter*, BBC Publications, 1977

Colbeck, John, *Pottery, the Technique of Throwing*, B. T. Batsford, 1969

Rhodes, Dan, *Pottery Form*, Pitman, 1978

Whitford and Wong, *Handmade Pottery Tools*, Kodansha

Decoration

Caiger Smith, Alan, *Tin Glaze Pottery in Europe and the Islamic World*, Faber and Faber, 1973

Mino, Yutaka, *Freedom of Clay and Brush through Seven Centuries in Northern China Tz'u-chou Type Wares, 960–1600 AD*, Indiana University Press

Phillips, Anthony, *Slips and Slipware*, B. T. Batsford, 1990

Shafer, Tom, *Pottery Decoration*, Pitman, 1976

Glazes

Cooper, Emmanuel, and Royle, Derek, *Glazes for the Studio Potter*, B. T. Batsford, 1978

Rhodes, Dan, *Clay and Glazes for the Potter*, Pitman, 1960

Rhodes, Dan, *Stoneware and Porcelain*, Pitman, 1960

Sutherland, Brian, *Glazes from Natural Sources: a working handbook for potters*, B. T. Batsford, 1987

Kilns

Byers, Ian, *Raku*, B. T. Batsford, 1990

Frazer, Harry, *Kilns and Kiln Firing for the Craft Potter*, Pitman, 1969

Gregory, Ian, *Kiln Building*, A. & C. Black, second edition 1984

Rhodes, Dan, *Kiln Design and Construction*, Pitman, 1968

Design

Clark, Garth, *American Potters: the work of twenty modern masters*, Watson Gupthill, 1981

Lane, Peter, *Studio Ceramics*, Collins, 1983

Street-Porter, Janet and Tim, *The British Teapot*, Angus and Robertson, 1981

General

Cooper, Emmanuel, *A History of World Pottery*, B.T. Batsford, 1981

Fournier, Robert, *Illustrated Dictionary of Pottery Form*, Van Nostrand Reinhold, 1981

Fournier, Robert, *Illustrated Dictionary of Practical Pottery*, Van Nostrand Reinhold, 1977

Leach, Bernard, *A Potter's Book*, Faber and Faber, 1940

59 Hand-built raku-fired and reduced pot by Glen Etienne, evolving from Egyptian studies

Magazines

American Ceramics, 15 West 44th Street, New York, NY 10036

American Craft (formerly *Craft Horizons*), American Crafts Council, 40 West 53rd Street, New York, NY 10019

Ceramic Review, Craftsmen Potters' Association, 21 Carnaby Street, London W1V 1PH

Ceramics Monthly, Colombus, Ohio 43212, USA

Crafts, Crafts Council, 44a Pentonville Road, London N1 9HF

Pottery in Australia, Potters' Society of Australia, 48 Burton Street, Darlinghurst, Sydney, New South Wales 2010

Studio Potter, PO Box 4954, Manchester NH 03108, USA

Museums to visit

In Britain

Ashmolean Museum of Art and Archaeology, Beaumont Street, Oxford
historic collection of fine art and crafts from many countries

British Museum, Great Russell Street, London WC1
historic treasures from many countries

Fitzwilliam Museum, Trumpington Street, Cambridge
historic collection of fine art and crafts from many countries

Gladstone Pottery Museum, Uttoxeter Road, Longton, Stroke-on-Trent, Staffordshire
working museum complete with original bottle kilns

Hunterian Museum, University of Glasgow, Glasgow, Scotland
modern museum housing a worldwide historic collection of art and crafts

Percival David Foundation of Chinese Art, 53 Gordon Square, London WC1
Chinese ceramics, mainly porcelain

Pitt Rivers Museum, Parks Road, Oxford
collection of craftwork from a variety of ancient cultures, including African

Victoria and Albert Museum, Cromwell Road, London SW7
the national museum for the decorative arts, including ceramics, costume, furniture, etc.

In America

American Craft Museum, 73 West 45th Street, New York, NY 10019

Cooper-Hewitt Museum of Decorative Arts and Design, 9 East 9th Street, New York, NY 100193

Everson Museum of Art, 401 Harrison Street, Syracuse, New York

Garth Clark Gallery, 5280 Wiltshire Boulevard, Los Angeles, California

Helen Drutt Gallery, 1721 Walnut Street, Philadelphia, Pennsylvania 19103

National Museum of American Art, Smithsonian Institution, Washington DC

Phoenix Art Museum, 1625 North Central Avenue, Phoenix, Arizona

Whitney Museum of American Art, 945 Madison Avenue, New York

Fig. 30 Detail from a painted cotton hanging, Kalamkari, Andra Pradesh

List of suppliers

In Britain

The Fulham Pottery, 8–10 Ingate Place, Battersea, London SW8 3NS, tel 071–720 0050

Moira Pottery Co Ltd (Raw Materials Dept), Moira, Burton-on-Trent, Staffs DE12 6DF, tel 0283 221 961

Potclays Ltd, Brick Kiln Lane, Etruria, Stoke-on-Trent, Staffs ST4 7BP, tel 0782 29816

Potterycrafts Ltd, Campbell Road, Shelton, Stoke-on-Trent, Staffs ST4 4ET, tel 0782 272444

In America

American Art Clay Co. Inc., 4717 West 16th Street, Indianapolis, IN 46222

Leslie Ceramics Supply Co., 1212 San Pable Ave, Berkeley, California 94706, tel (415) 524–7363

Miami Clay Co., 270 N. E. 183rd Street, Miami, Florida 33179, tel (305) 266–6024

Minnesota Clay, 8001 Grand Avenue, South Bloomington, Minnesota 55420, tel (612) 884–9101

60 *Tileworks at the Guiliao Commune, Gwangtung Province, China, 1978*

Index